The Menace of Rape and Domestic Violence

Author: Shabbir H M Tankiwala

The power to manipulate beliefs is all that matters most, because we humans live with beliefs and it is always easy to manipulate beliefs.

Article title "**Woman and Her Significance in the Universe(10),**" has written: "Woman is first created by man's will, he dominates her and changes her whole being (hypnotism). Here is the explanation of the relation of the psychical to the physical in man and woman. Man assumes a reciprocal action of body and mind, in the sense rather that the dominant mind creates the body, than that the mind merely projects itself on phenomena, whilst the woman accepts both mental and psychical phenomena empirically. Man not only forms himself, but woman also a far easier matter.

In order to perceive and apperceive the special form, matter must not itself be formless, woman's relation to man, however, is nothing but that of matter to form, and her comprehension of him nothing but willingness to be as much formed as possible by him, the instinct of those without existence for existence. Furthermore, this "comprehension" is not theoretical, it is not sympathetic, it is only a desire to be sympathetic; it is importunate and egoistical."………

It is quite erroneous to suppose that woman has an innate capacity to understand the individuality of a man. The lover, who is so easily fooled by the unconscious simulation of a deeper comprehension on the part of his sweetheart, may believe that he understands himself through a girl, but those who are less easily satisfied cannot help seeing that women only possess a sense of the fact not of the individuality of the soul, only for the formal general fact, not for the differentiation of the personality.

In this life we do not see things very clearly. We are constantly faced with contradictions. Though we know what is right, we have trouble doing it. Our thoughts soar high, but our actions cannot rise to the level of our thoughts. The world is full of misery and injustice; as quickly as we remove some, more seems to rush in to take its place.

Rape as a weapon of war is seen as one of the great mass crimes of modern times with it adding its own brand of shame to wars. From conflicts in Bosnia to Uganda thousands of women and girls have been victims to this traumatising crime, with many of these rapes leading to victims being murdered or committing suicide.

It's more about the shared assumptions about masculinity and sexuality that makes it such a powerful weapon that soldiers use without necessarily having been given orders.

Dating as far back as the Japanese occupation of Nanking in 1937, rape as a weapon of war has been prevalent in conflicts throughout the 1990s and continues to be used today. A common misconception is that rape is simply a by-product of war. Sexual violence is certainly occurring in every conflict around the world but its role has evolved from an unfortunate effect of war to a tactic used to humiliate and control entire populations.

Rape as weapon of war, is not something new, for ages such heinous crime has been committed against women, in the 1990's when the erstwhile Yugoslavia got disintegrated and the various region of it plunged into bloody civil war, some of the most horrific crimes were committed against women in Bosnia by the Serbian forces, when Sex terror was unleashed on them, it has been reported that many Muslim women were brutally Raped by the Serb forces and to add to the misery of beleaguered women and to their dismay most of these women were allegedly rape in front of their Father, brothers, husband and children.

In Bosnia "Women were raped so they could give birth to a Serbian baby." The same tactic was used in a "very strategic attack" by state-backed Pakistani troops during the fight for Bangladesh's independence in 1971. Whether a woman is raped at gunpoint or trafficked into sexual slavery by an occupying force, the sexual abuse will shape not just her own but her community's future for years to come.

There are testimonies from Bosnian women who had soldiers tell them, while raping them, that they wanted to get them pregnant or force them to have children who would look ethnically different from their mother, or that they were raping them to punish them for being Muslim (or Croatian). There were also women who became pregnant and were forced to carry their babies to term.

Genocidal rape against the **Bosniak** (Bosnian Muslim) ethnic group. Estimates of the total number of women raped during the war range from 12,000 to 50,000. The **International Criminal Tribunal for the former Yugoslavia** (ICTY) declared that "systematic rape", and "sexual enslavement" in time of war was a **crime against humanity**, second only to the **war crime** of genocide. Although the ICTY did not treat the mass rapes as genocide, it is clear from the organized, and systematic nature of the mass rapes of the Bosniak female population, that these rapes were a part of a larger campaign of genocide. While women of all ethnic groups were affected by instances of rape during the conflict, the great majority of war crimes were perpetrated by the Bosnian Serb forces and Serb paramilitary units, who used rape as an instrument of terror as part of their programme of ethnic cleansing.

Violence against women, especially rape, has added its own brand of shame to recent wars. From conflicts in Bosnia and Herzegovina to Peru to Rwanda, girls and women have been singled out for rape, imprisonment, torture and execution. Rape, identified by psychologists as the most intrusive of traumatic events, has been documented in many armed conflicts including those in Bangladesh, Cambodia, Cyprus, Haiti, Liberia, Somalia and Uganda.

Systematic rape is often used as a weapon of war in 'ethnic cleansing'. More than 20,000 Muslim girls and women have been raped in Bosnia since fighting began in April 1992, according to a European Community fact-finding team. Teenage girls have been a particular target in Bosnia and Herzegovina and Croatia, according to "The State of the World's Children 1996 report." The report also says that impregnated girls have been forced to bear 'the enemy's' child.

Myanmar's transition to democracy following five decades of brutal military rule has won widespread international praise, but rights' groups say little has changed in resource-rich border areas, where the army continues to grapple with stubborn ethnic insurgencies. As in the past, the use of sexual violence against civilians is widespread and systematic.

"Rights activists in Myanmar, also known as Burma, say the army continues to use rape as a weapon of war nearly three years after President Thein Sein's nominally civilian government ended a half-century of brutal military rule. The Women's League of Burma released a report documenting more than 100 rapes, almost all in townships plagued by stubborn ethnic insurgencies. Nearly half were brutal gang rapes, several of the victims were children, and 28 of the women were killed or died from their injuries, as confirmed by "Tin Tin Nyo, the Women league's general secretary."

Rape and sexual abuse are not just a by-product of war but are used as a deliberate military strategy, it says. The opportunistic rape and pillage of previous centuries has been replaced in modern conflict by rape used as an orchestrated combat tool.

According to RAINN.org, there are approximately 237,868 victims (age 12 or older) of sexual assault each year. Every 2 minutes an American is sexually assaulted... and 1 out of every 6 American women has been the victim of an attempted or completed rape in her lifetime. These are disgusting, but, unfortunate facts.

While the history of wars and conflicts is replete with systematic incidents of sexual violence against vulnerable women, modern-day wars have witnessed large-scale indiscriminate deployment of rape as a "weapon" of war by combatants. In recent armed conflicts — such as in the former Yugoslavia, Liberia, the Democratic Republic of the Congo, Sudan, the Central African Republic, Sierra Leone and Rwanda — the widespread use of rape as a tool of warfare has become a conspicuous phenomenon.

Rape is the most powerful, cost-effective weapon available for destroying the lives of "enemy" women, families, and entire communities, demoralizing enemy forces, and, in some cases, accomplishing genocide. Rape is being used more than any other prohibited weapon of war including starvation, attacks on cultural objects; and the use of herbicides, biological or chemical weapons, dum-dum bullets, white phosphorus or blinding lasers.

Rape has been a dishonourable camp follower of war for as long as armies have marched into battle. In the 20th century, perceptions of rape in war have moved from something that is inevitable when men are deprived of female companionship for prolonged periods to an actual tactic in conflict. The lasting psychological harm that rape inflicts on its victims has also been recognized: Rape is always torture, says Manfred Nowak, Special Rapporteur on torture and other cruel, inhuman or degrading treatment or punishment.

"Soeren Kern published an article about child sex slavery in the UK. He focuses on a report about the large-scale "grooming" of non-Muslim girls age between 11&16 by gangs of Muslim men into sex slavery. These men do not prey upon Muslim girls. The government, police force, and media have been "multi-culturally correct" and very reluctant to expose this phenomenon or to charge these men. Many feminists would say that men all over the world buy and sell women, kidnap or trick them into prostitution. And they are right. But they are wrong to refuse to focus on Paedophelia Sex Slavery wherever and whenever this monster rears its ugly head. The prepared report is meticulous. It documents that "officials in England and Wales were aware of rampant child grooming—the process by which sexual predators befriend and build trust with children in order to prepare them for abuse—by Muslim gangs since at least 1988."

Imagine that. Imagine being a young girl abused and the very people you are told will help you close their doors on you and worse still blames you for the abuse! The young women concerned are often seen by the Police as being deviant or promiscuous. The adult men with whom they are seen with are not questioned.

These accounts give us a harrowing perspective of the scale of the problem. How do we safeguard young vulnerable girls from those who want to exploit them? How do we inform the public to recognise a child who is being groomed? What use is all of this if the authorities are not going to help bring perpetrators to justice?

In Article **"When the rapist is a she,"** has written; "But the notion that a woman cannot rape a man has been around for quite a while and still persists. In the late '1970s it was argued in the book "Sex, Crime and the Law" that "for obvious biological reasons, a woman cannot be guilty of raping a man ... certainly a woman cannot bring about sexual intercourse with a male against his will." What's certain is actually the opposite, that it's physiologically possible for a woman to impregnate herself by raping a man. (Also, note that rape doesn't have to include penis-in-vagina penetration.) Researchers have studied this very thing, in fact. A study in the Archives of Sexual Behaviour found that "the belief that it is impossible for males to respond sexually when subjected to sexual molestation by women is contradicted" and it also corroborated "previous research indicating that male sex response can occur in a variety of emotional states, including anger and terror." Much as woman can experience lubrication and even achieve orgasm during rape, men's physiological response can act independent of consent or desire — and in neither case does it make it any less rape-y.".........

Not just women, but, Male gender is not spared as well, there are many incidents of men being raped and sexually tortured during wars, also when men's are held as prisoner of war; The facts of brutality men experiences during captivity are horrific, with reports of men not just being raped, but systematically raped by large group of men, repeatedly and resolutely, to deliberately maximize the physical and mental damage. Sexual violence against men is used as a weapon of war around the world, not just in Africa but in past conflicts in Bosnia, Iran, Chile... Surveys of political prisoners, from Sarajevo to El Salvador, have reported up to 80 per cent of male prisoners having been raped.

During the wars in Bosnia and Croatia in the early "19' Nineties," male rape and sexual torture were used as a weapon of war with serious consequences for the victims' mental, physical, and sexual health, Balkan experts says.

Despite the fact that hundreds of Bosnian men are believed to be victims of wartime rapes and sexual abuse, only two non-governmental organisations in Bosnia with limited resources provide them with psychological help. Their status has not been properly regulated by law either. "Men were forced to have sexual intercourse in front of other inmates. This, of course, caused them great physical and psychological pain."

According to testimonies of some of Bosnian war crime victims, the victims were sexually assaulted with glass bottles, guns and truncheons. Also, castrations were allegedly performed by crude means - such as forcing other detainees to bite off a prisoner's testicles. The witnesses also said that prisoners had been forced to commit other types of abuse on each other, and several men made statements that fathers and sons had been coerced into performing sexual acts upon each other.

When a crime doesn't exist in the eyes of the law, there's little support, protection or justice. But it's also the shame that stops many men from reporting what happened to them. "It's a taboo in civil society for a man to admit he's been raped. "There's confusion from people about the difference between sexual violence and homosexuality.

It's this stigma that makes male rape such a difficult subject to shine a light on. It's extremely difficult to get people to talk; There are very high levels of shame and a very high fear of stigmatization around people's masculinity, being seen as not a 'real man'. When women get raped, the accusation is that they've become prostitutes. With men, it's that they've become homosexuals or women.

Sexual violence in the Democratic Republic of Congo (DRC) is endemic. Abuses are committed by government forces, including la Police Nationale Congolaise (the PNC), and the rebel groups FARDC and FDLR. Rape often forms part of a larger terror campaign where victims are subjected to looting and torture.

According to preliminary results from the International Men and Gender Equality Survey (IMAGES) **more than one in three Men** surveyed in the Democratic Republic of the Congo's war-torn east **admits committing sexual assault**, and three in four believe that a woman who "does not dress decently is asking to be raped". Impunity for these crimes is the norm, few cases are prosecuted and few perpetrators face justice. However, stigmatization and being ostracized from family members and the community are daily realities for survivors.

Men aren't simply raped, they are forced to penetrate holes in banana trees that run with acidic sap, to sit with their genitals over a fire, to drag rocks tied to their penis, to give oral sex to queues of soldiers, to be penetrated with screwdrivers and sticks. Because there has been so little research into the rape of men during war, it's not possible to say with any certainty why it happens or even how common it is – although a rare 2010 survey, published in the *Journal of the American Medical Association*, found that 22% of men and 30% of women in Eastern Congo reported conflict-related sexual violence.

The research by Lara Stemple at the University of California doesn't only show that male sexual violence is a component of wars all over the world, it also suggests that international aid organisations are failing male victims. Her study cites a review of 4,076 NGOs that have addressed wartime sexual violence. Only 3% of them mentioned the experience of men in their literature. "Typically," Stemple says, "as a passing reference."

That men are victims of sexual assault should not come as news to feminists, especially because it is observed so frequently in prisons, and I also doubt that many feminists deny that women perpetrators of sexual assault against men exist and contribute to the male rape victim demographic. However, the fact that men frequently under-report rape (especially when perpetrated by a woman, but in general), and are less likely to recognize an incident of forcible sex as rape due to stigma, does little to help the cause.

Further, patriarchal attitudes, which are frequently credited with perpetuating female rape culture, are also responsible for the same problems that contribute to the problematic marginalization of male rape. Male-centric ideas, such as that men are stronger than women and cannot be victimized by them, simultaneously cause male privilege in society and male oppression in the context of sexual consent. The harm that these myths do to male victims of sexual assault cannot be overstated, and if men should oppose the patriarchy for no other reason, then at least they ought to consider the harm they do to themselves by perpetuating such ideas. The patriarchy hurts men and women alike, but in very different ways, and the ways in which it hurts men are insidious and subtle.

In twenty-first century the so-called "Arab Spring" conflict has proved to become the mother of all wars ever since the end of 2nd world-war that ended in 1940s.

"Arab spring" is the name given by the western media to the Revolutionary Movement, a struggle that started in the year 2011 by the suppressed Arab citizens to seek liberal and better quality of life and freedom of speech, demanding democratic and civil rights, the protest demonstration for freedom from dictatorial regimes that first started in a small town of Tunisia soon spread to many Arabian Peninsula and few North-African countries. But, what seemingly started in earnest as a full blown peaceful protest to seek democratic rights in which both men and women equally participated to demonstrate against the authoritarian regime in countries like Libya, Egypt, Yemen and Tunisia etc, but, no sooner had the struggle started. The whole concept of revolutionary movement was hijacked and twisted and turned into full blown communal and sectarian violence, by taking deliberate advantage of generation old bitter rivalry amongst various religious and ethnic communities in Islamic world by many alleged state sponsor groups of extremist Islamic fundamentalist forces.

The Salafist belonging to Sunni-Muslim fundamentalist jihadist groups turned the Arab spring protest into full fledge sectarian and communal conflict, to achieve their selfish objective the Islamic jihadist groups like the most notorious amongst them "ISIS, Al-Qaeda, Al-Nusra and BOKO Haram," started to terrorise people and cause havoc in the civil society, the monstrous Islamic elements brutally started enforcing their insular outdated chemistry of extreme hard-core Islamic religious practice on common people.

Particularly hard pressed are the women belonging to almost every religious and racial communities. The Islamic militants brazenly intimidate folks belonging to almost all Non Sunni Muslim communities, and even members of Sunni-Islam especially those people who are liberal and secular are not spared, the Islamic jihadist terrorists browbeats even the Sunni-Muslim folks who are secular and liberal of dire consequence if they do not follow the strict Islamic law and abide by it, these jihadist groups have not hesitated even in raping and killing Sunni-Muslims those who dare to oppose their diktat.

In the Arab spring conflict the Islamic militants have reserved their harsh brutality for Non-Sunni Muslims, they are fierce and callous when it comes to dealing with civilians belonging to communities such as the Shia's, Christians, Kurdish, Jewish, Yazidi's etc, the various Sunni-Muslim jihadist ostentatiously loots wealth, ferociously rapes women.

A new concept has emerged in the Arab Spring conflict **"SEX – JIHAD"** something unheard of by even the staunch Sunni-Muslim religious leaders as well, when some of the Salafist clerics belonging to Sunni Islam sect, made appeal to young Sunni Muslim women and girls to participate in jihad in a unique way and to play a role in establishing the Islamic caliphate in Iraq, Syria, Jordan and Lebanon, the appeal to the girls and women of Muslim community was to participate in jihad by surrendering their bodies to appease and to soothe the minds of the jihadist by sleeping with them.

The extremist group ISIS (Islamic state of Iraq & Al-sham) owing allegiance to "Sunni–Islam" has been wreaking havoc across the Middle-East Arabian countries in what is largely communal conflict between two prominent Islamic Sect, with waging war showing no sign of abating, Their (ISISI) latest savage demand is sure to send shock-wave throughout the civilized world – **"hand us over your young daughters/widows for sex jihad, or else."**

The Islamic Supreme Council of America defines a fatwa as an "Islamic legal pronouncement, issued by an expert in religious law (mufti)," pertaining to a specific issue, usually at the request of an individual or judge to resolve an issue where Islamic jurisprudence (fiqh), is unclear." Thus, the radicals in the ISIS organization have taken the pronouncement permitting Jihad al-Nikah (jihad of legal copulation) very seriously.

The militant Islamist group ISIS (the Islamic State in Iraq and Syria) put up posters calling on the people of Mosul to bring forward for them their unmarried girls to participate in *"Jihad al-Nikah,"* or sex jihad. The reports came from Al-

Masryalyoum, a well-respected Egyptian daily newspaper as well as other sources in the Arab press.

ISIS after gaining control over vast territories in northern Iraq including Mosul, Iraq's second largest city. *Jihad al-Nikah* refers to women joining the jihad by offering sex to the male fighters.

Posters in public places in Mosul read:

"We call upon the people of this county to bring their unmarried girls so they can fulfil their duty in sex jihad for their warrior brothers in the city and anyone who will not appear will feel the full force of the sharia [Islamic law] upon him/her."

ISIS fighters are ordering terrified families in Iraq to hand over their daughters for sex. Leaflets in the captured cities of Mosul and Tikrit claim the women – virgins or not – must join Jihad, or Holy war, and cleanse themselves by sleeping with militants.

The consequences of refusal to submit to sex jihad are beatings or death. The Jihad al-Nikah often incorporates beatings and transference to many different men for all sorts of sexual acts. Leaflets distributed in the Iraqi cities tell families that they must hand over their daughters for sex jihad, and that "**those that refuse** to do so are violating God's will."

Jihad al-Nikah, (Jihad al-Nikah is an Arabic phrase meaning "sexual holy war,") permitting extramarital sexual relations with multiple partners, is considered by some hard-line Sunni Muslim Salafists as a legitimate form of holy war.

Reports emanated from Mosul indicated that ISIS fighters resorted to going door-to-door, entering houses, killing the men and raping the women. Al-Iraqiya TV station published a report about the story of two Iraqi girls who were raped by the armed men of ISIS in Mosul. The two girls, who are sisters, reportedly said that ISIS fighters came into their house, killed the male members of the family and afterwards, they took it in turns of raping the women.

So, Technically known as a *Jihad al-Nika'h* (often translated as Sexual Holy War or Holy War of Prostitution), highly renown Saudi cleric Sheikh Mohamad bin Abdul Rahman al-Arefe, Chief Imam of the Mosque of the King Fahd Academy of the Royal Saudi Navy issued a fatwa (Islamic theological ruling) authorizing girls as young as 14 to step forward to make sacrifices in the name of Islamic Jihad. Among the sacrifices expected of the women and girls was they surrender "their chastity" as well as "their dignity" as reported by the Assyrian International News Service on June 24, 2013. Considering Jihad al-Nika'h as a legitimate form of holy war, Sunni-Muslim women and girls from Britain, Iraq, Malaysia and Australia have reportedly volunteered to offer themselves in "temporary marriages," usually lasting only as long as it take for an ISIS jihadists to sexually gratify themselves.

Many young girls and women from countries such as Somalia, Tunisia, Egypt as well from affluent European countries like Britain, France and Netherland, heeded to the call given by the Islamic clerics and willingly surrendered their body for what these girls perceived as mandatory holy duty, and travelled to countries like Syria and Iraq and slept or still are with cunning jihadist men.

Records have also proved that Australian, British, and Malaysian Sunni Muslim women travelled to Iraq and Syria to participate in Jihad al-Nikah, or sexual jihad, and willingly joined Islamic State (ISIS) terrorists. They intended to becoming comfort women for the jihadists as the Sunni men continue to establish a Caliphate in Iraq and Syria. "These women are believed to have offered themselves in sexual comfort roles to ISIS fighters who are attempting to establish Islamic rule in the Mid-east," said one source in Malaysia, further adding, "This concept may seem controversial but it has arisen because certain Muslim women here (Malaysia) are showing sympathy for the ISIS struggle." "Checks with our foreign counterparts and intelligence disseminated reveal that there may be up to 50 Malaysians women in the Middle East."

Over 600 British Muslims are believed to be fighting for "ISIS" in the conflict in Syria and Iraq. The number also includes "British Muslim women who are not fighting on the front line, but are still involved by performing sexual jihad", confirms the intelligence official.

In Britain and the Netherlands, where Muslim gangs have been involved in targeting teenage girls for sex, drugs, gang-rape and child sex slavery 'Love Jihad' transforms into 'Sex Jihad'. Vulnerable Sikh girls were apparently targets of Muslim gangs in the 1980s, and White teenagers in the last 15 years. The scandal never came to light due to the political correctness of the British police force and the media, which found it difficult to name the culprits for fear of being accused of racism. But apart from political correctness, virulent patriarchy is the villain in 'Sex Jihad', too. Women are the only victims here.

'Love Jihad' and 'Sex Jihad' are thus tussles between two or more patriarchies.-

Most of these young Sunni Muslim girls who offered their bodies to be consumed by the terrorist, it has been reported that many of these girls and women apart from unwanted pregnancy they have contracted several Sex related ailments some are believed to have even contracted Aids "HIV."

The high risk of infection with sexually transmitted diseases (STDs), including HIV/AIDS, accompanies either to those girls who voluntarily surrender their bodies for Sex – Jihad or all other types of sexual violence against women and girls. The movement of refugees and marauding military units and the breakdown of health services and public education worsens the impact of diseases and chances for treatment. For example, one study has suggested that the exchange of sex for protection during the civil war in Uganda in the 1980s was a contributing factor to the country's high rate of AIDS.

One striking difference between the use of rape as a weapon of war in pre-1990 conflicts and in latter-day wars is the emergence and "wilful" transmission of HIV to the victims. Serious questions have been raised in the social science literature about the actual time of transmission and infection, and whether the "intent" of the perpetrators could conclusively be to infect the victim with HIV. Nonetheless, there is evidence from the victims' accounts confirming the deliberate nature of these acts.

One bizarre narrative of an alleged incident that has been reported from Kenya (the identity of the victim and that of the allege perpetrator has been concealed by the authorities for obvious reason), wherein a young Kenyan woman was brutally raped by a man, the young woman a student had allegedly gone to a club to attend a party, the girl had enjoyed a couple of drinks during the party, when she returned back to her hostel room under influence of alcohol, taking advantage of the woman state of mind a cruel man not only raped that young woman to satisfy his sex desire but he outrageously and deliberately infected the young woman whom he raped with "HIV," then, as a consequence of being raped, what the victim of rape the frustrated young woman did could be termed as equally inhuman, the young girl infected with HIV, she decided to take revenge for her lost dignity and chastity with entire male gender. To seek revenge, She started sleeping with as many men (its reported, 300+) as possibly she could and its alleged that she had unprotected sex, therefore most men with whom the young beleaguered woman slept with and had sex with, those unfortunate men "have or may potentially have" got infected with "HIV' Aids."

Now, what the young woman did to seek revenge for being raped and infected with HIV, it raises one pressing question, what do the scholars and intellectuals would have to say, about the action of beleaguered woman? Is it OK? If someone Mess up your life. You Mess up others life. Is it a fair thing to do? Is it morally correct to ruin other innocent lives because someone else has destroyed your life? No, Never, at least I firmly believe, under duress or frustration don't mess up and please don't harm others life. What do y'all think?

The impact of violence and bloody wars severely devastates women, large scale violence traumatizes women living in a conflict zone which leads to a variety of physical and social problems. During conflicts, women are more exposed to insecurity because they are pre-occupied with their children and cannot conveniently run away to safety. Conflict destroys the safe environment provided by a house and a family, leads to inadequate nutrition, education and unemployment. Stress, trauma, depression, spontaneous abortions and miscarriages becomes all too common.

Women who are victims of rape during conflicts have an inalienable right to reparation, psychological and physical rehabilitation, needs access to social measures, and health security. In efforts to reconstruct post-conflict societies, the disarmament, demobilization and reintegration (DDR) processes should include sustainable policies and programmes aimed at holistic reparation for victims of rape during wars and conflicts.

Like other forms of sexual assault, responding to sexual terrorism requires criminal justice, medical, psychological and social initiatives. However, in many cases the girls or women are too scared to come forward for treatment, which hinders efforts to tackle the problem. Despite this, some progress has been made.

Some call it 'rape jihad', others opt for 'sexual terrorism' or 'forced marriage'. Whatever one may choose to call it, when terrorism meets sexual violence it is two crimes too many. It is the use of sexual abuse to spread terror with the intention of controlling or manipulating the government or parts of a population. By intimidating and humiliating families, terrorists hope to exert influence over their targeted audience.

Sexual terrorism is often classified as being gendered in nature, due to the fact that the victims are chiefly girls or women. In sexual terrorism, the rape or assault is part of a broader objective: to spread terror or send a message, a motivation similar to that found in the use of suicide bombings. The perpetrators justify sexual terrorism by claiming that the Prophet Mohammed sanctioned the rape of both non-Muslims (infidels or *kafirs*) and Muslims who do not adhere strictly to Islam.

In August 2013, a young mother in Somalia was kidnapped and raped by members of the terrorist network Al-Shabaab for being a Christian. The terrorists contacted the victim's husband, warning him to convert to Islam. Human Rights Watch has released similar reports on a spate of child kidnappings in Somalia. The kidnapped children were trained to fight and used to protect the adult terrorists. According to the reports, the girls were forced to marry these 'soldiers' or face beheading, after which their heads would be sent back to their schools as a warning against insolence.

In one of the many notorious incident of Sex – Jihad, a 16 year old Syrian girl by the name of "Rawan Milad Al-dah" was rescued from sexual slavery by the Syrian soldiers loyal to its president Assad, the hard-pressed girl "Rawan" took courage to share her ordeal with a TV broadcaster. She was brave enough to keep her face straight while talking about her being sold to the "Rebel free Syrian army terrorist" by her own father as a sex slave in the name of jihad, but do I doubt that the jihadist would use rape as weapon of war in the conflict stricken country like Syria? Not one bit.

ISIS has received considerable world attention for its savage beheadings, executions of captured soldiers and men in conquered towns and villages, violence against Christians and Shiites, and the destruction of non-Sunni shrines and places of worship. But its barbarity against women has been treated as a side issue. Arab and Muslim governments, vocal on the threat ISIS poses to regional stability, have been virtually silent on ISIS's systemic degradation, abuse, and humiliation of women. To the men of ISIS, women are an inferior race, to be enjoyed for sex and be discarded, or to be sold off as slaves. From ISIS-captured territory in Syria, appeared a photograph of a line of women, covered from head to toe and tied to one another by a rope, as they were being led to a makeshift slave market. Little girls, who were going to school and playing with dolls before ISIS fighters arrived at their doorstep, were married off to men many times their age.

Article title "**The Federalist: Sex slaves in Islamic State**" wrote; "Members of the all-women al-Khanssaa Brigade in Raqqa, Syria, are running brothels for Islamic State murderers. British female jihadis are running brothels full of women kidnapped and **forced into sex slavery** by Islamic State militants. It is understood they are members of an ultra-religious IS 'police' force' tasked with looking after girls captured from the Yazidi tribe in Iraq. As many as 3,000 Iraqi women have been taken captive in the last two weeks by the terror group. Sources suggest that members of the all-women al-Khanssaa Brigade in Raqqa, Syria, are running brothels to satisfy the fighters' desires. One said: "These women are using barbaric interpretations of the Islamic faith to justify their actions. "They believe the militants can use these women as they please as they are non-Muslims. "The

Yazidi people are being ethnically cleansed, and their women are being subjected to the most brutal treatment. "It is the British women who have risen to the top of the Islamic State's **sharia police** and now they are in charge of this operation. "It is as bizarre as it is perverse." A report obtained by the Daily Mirror from researchers at think tank MEMRI – the Middle East Media Research Institution – confirms ethnic sex slavery is taking place on a massive scale. The report states: "During its takeover of large parts of northern Iraq the IS captured many Yazidi villages, and reportedly took many Yazidi women to be sold and used as sex slaves."......................

According to Hanafi jurist Imam al Sarakhsi (d. 1090), the Prophet Mohammed called upon jihadists to "kill the warring elders of the pagans and to keep alive their subordinates." Al Sarakhsi defines the subordinates as women and small children whom he stresses are supposed to be taken as captives, according to Islamic law. The essential problem with ISIS is that they take such teachings to the extreme. They don't just kill the "warring elders." They slaughter in the most brutal fashion imaginable every man who doesn't think like them, whether he be Yazidi, Turcoman, Christian, Shabak, Shia, or even a Sunni who doesn't buy into their extremist worldview. They behead, torture, and even crucify people, displaying the dead bodies afterwards in a barbaric fashion.

Regarding the women of their opponents, they don't merely take them captive. They massively rape them, enslave them, and force them to convert to Islam, even though the Quran clearly states "there is no compulsion in religion." As many as 1,500 Yazidis and Christians women and girls in Iraq may have been forced into sex slavery and human trafficking, the UN reports. The UN also stresses that brutal rapes have systematically been used as a weapon of war by ISIS against Yazidi, Turcoman, Christian, and Shabak community members in Iraq.

Thousands of Iraq's Yazidis community, who are driven from their homes by ISIS and trapped in the desperate siege of Mt. Sinjar, have captured the world's attention and received some relief from U.S. airstrikes and humanitarian aid. But hundreds of Yazidi women taken by ISIS and held in a secret prison where they have been raped and sold off like property are facing an equally dire fate.

Survivors who managed to escape from ISIS, said that the women held in its prison in Mosul face two fates: Those who convert to Islam are sold as brides to Islamist fighters for prices as low as US$25 and ranging up to $150. Those who do not convert face daily rape and a slow death. Accounts of the prison have come from women those who managed to cleverly hide their cellular phones, and called their relatives to describe their plight.

In the late 80s there was a commercial, "This is your brain on drugs", that gave the example of your brain as an egg, drugs as a hot frying pan and your brain being fried on drugs. Well, it turns out that it's far worse than drugs. Islam's hateful rhetoric in a woman's mind makes the 18″ drop into the heart, and infects the very soul of a woman. She begins to abandon characteristics that are inherent to her gender like: Compassion, kindness, mercy, empathy and sympathy. A woman's nature is to nurture…that is, until Islam beats a woman senseless. Islam's dictates fester in a man till acted out against women…and women see little to no worth in themselves. And, apparently, when a woman is subjected to this misogynistic creed long enough…she joins the dark side.

It's not unusual for rape to be used as a weapon of war, but this is one of the first indications of the extent it has been used in Libya, since staggeringly beautiful young woman "Miss Iman al-Obedi" burst into the hotel housing the foreign journalists in Tripoli in March 2011 and she accused pro-Gaddafi militiamen of gang-raping her. In Libya rape was extensively and profoundly used by the soldiers loyal to Libyan dictator Muammar Gaddafi, there are stories of sex materials like Viagra and condoms being found from the dead bodies of Gaddafi's soldiers. Unprecedented numbers of sex crimes were committed by forces loyal to Gaddafi, women and young girls and boys as well were ferociously raped in Libya.

Article title "Sexual Terror: Untold Stories of Beslan Jihad" ------ "On September 1, 2004, Islamist terrorist sent by the Chechen terrorist warlord Shamil Basayev, the terrorists stormed a school in Beslan, Russia, and perpetrated one of the most heinous terror attacks in history. Though many people may have heard of this attack, it is very likely that most do not know what really happened there. The reality is so dark that few dare speak of what went on.

There are predators in wait lurking everywhere searching for unsuspecting victims. If a person has a proclivity or a secret desire, that inclination can easily come out if an opportunity arises. And that is what happened at Beslan. The terrorists immediately killed the men because they wanted no resistance for their plans. Then, when they saw the helpless girls in front of them, the temptation became too much. Their perverse dreams came true.

Beslan was clearly a sexual homicide/sexual suicide. That is, the offenders wanted more than simple terrorism. Some of the terrorists at Beslan were hired guns who did not plan on dying that day. They had not thought things through and did not realize that the Russians would not let them out alive. Then, once they were inside, and the realization dawned on them, plans changed.

Things had deteriorated when the media reported that there were only 354 victims. Wanting to have a dramatic impact, the terrorists exploded with anger. There were 1200 victims, and the Russians were trying to down play the incident. The terrorists said they would have to eliminate victims to fit with what the media had reported. Their demeanour worsened, and they got really mean.

It was then that they began raping the girls. They wanted sex as they killed, and this is sexual homicide. A sex killer gets excited when he thinks about forcing himself inside an unwilling victim, but the rape itself does not produce the ultimate excitement. It is the rape followed by the killing that is arousing. This is what happened at Beslan. One by one, females were targeted. The sex killers looked for the perfect victims, and after zeroing in, they grabbed and disrobed the little girls in the middle of the gym. There were muffled cries as the girls were humiliated in front of everyone. They were stripped, raped, and sodomized by several men Not content to simply rape, the terrorists used their guns and other objects to penetrate the screaming victims while the other hostages were forced to watch. And the terrorists laughed. They laughed as they violated the children and made them bleed. What few people know is that some of the girls died as a result of being raped with objects."--------------

In Egypt as well the story is no different, instead in the land of pharaohs, its sexual harassment record against women and girls particularly is worse as compare to many other Arab countries. It has been reported that many women and girls participating in pro-democracy movement to gain better civil rights for themselves, but, their participation in most of the pro-democracy (between 2011-2013) protest turned into unforgiving nightmares, horror struck when miscreant men mobbed up and molested and sexually harassed many Egyptian women and girls, the unruly mob didn't stopped at just molesting, but they even went step further at Cairo's famous Tahrir square raped few women in full public view, not just that Egyptian women and girls suffered the menace but few of the foreign journalist travelling to Egypt on assignment to report and cover events of political turmoil in Egypt were not spare either, at least three foreign journalist on separate occasion were either rape or brutally molested by mob of cruel men, these female journalist were doing their duty of reporting unravelling political events.

On the first anniversary of the election of President Mohamed Morsi on June 30-2013, thousands of Egyptians took to the streets in Tahrir Square in Cairo demanding the resignation of Mr Morsi. During the four days of protests, at least 91 women were attacked and sexually assaulted by mobs, while government leaders and police stood by and failed to intervene. Some women required extensive medical surgery after being subjected to brutal gang rapes and sexual assault with sharp objects. After the protests, survivors came forward to tell their horrific stories and demanded better security protection for women. While the protests led to the end of Morsi's presidency, the government downplayed the violence, prompting international calls to improve law enforcement and bring perpetrators to justice. These actions proved fruitless, as security forces again came under fire in August for using live ammunition against citizens resulting in 638 deaths.

Egypt's neighbouring countries in Africa are equally hit by Islamic fundamentalist ideology, one of the biggest country in Africa both economically and in population **Nigeria** is suffering excruciating pain of Islamic extremism, Nigeria based hard-line barbaric Sunni-Muslim terrorist group "Boko Haram" has been attacking civilians and local authorities with increasing vigour. The killings, torture, rape, other forms of sexual violence and abductions, crimes perpetrated by this criminal group against civilians have forced thousands of Nigerians to flee across the borders to seek refuge in neighbouring countries.

Similar to the Taliban in Afghanistan and Pakistan, and the Al-Shabaab group in Somalia, Boko Haram preaches radical Islam, it makes young girls its prime target. Its members pillage and burn schools to the ground, abducts female pupils, to "save them from sin", sells them as slaves, force them into marriage and treat them as trophies of war. Their criminal and misogynous policy aims to deprive women of their basic rights to life, security and education. These atrocities takes place within a context of widespread human rights violations in the Northern parts of Nigeria.

Terrorism in Nigeria, though it is a recent phenomenon, is assuming a dangerous trend with the Islamist terrorist group Boko Haram sect targeting children especially girls and women as weapons for their agitations. In February 2014, over 49 young boys in their boarding school were brutally murdered in a gruesome attack at night in Yobe State, North Eastern part of Nigeria. A few months' earlier, 27 girls and women were abducted by the Boko Haram.

In April 2014, about 270 school girls were abducted in Chibok Borno State in Nigeria and are reported to be sold into sexual slavery by the Boko Haram sect. Since the horrific incident, Boko Haram has periodically abducted more girls and women and killed defenceless boys and men under the pretext of propagating Islamic Religion and opposition to western style of education.

In most part of the world's Socially Conservative society homosexuality is considered as Sin, many of the prominent religions as well do not accept homosexuality. Hence, Gay and lesbian men and women particularly in Muslim dominated countries are distinctly most susceptible to brutal sexual violence. Gay men's have to constantly listen abuses and taunts and are consistently humiliated and raped. Gay men in Muslim countries find themselves untenable hence suffers severe discrimination. A men who is gay and is serving a jail sentence in countries like Pakistan, Syria or Egypt or even Uganda for instance is most certainly likely to be raped and physically abused by other serving inmates as well more likely by the police itself. Many gays and lesbian men and women from countries like Turkey, Lebanon or Egypt escapes from their country and migrates to more socially progressive countries for example "Germany or Sweden" in search for safe harbour, but most of these unfortunates gays and lesbians do not often find peace even in the socially progressive western countries as well, they have to suffer many peculiar types of harassment and sexual exploitation.

The prison cells of developed and socially progressive countries either are not safe for gays, lesbians or transgender, even in USA and European prisons the gay men are sexually discriminated. In prison rape, the perpetrator and victim are almost always the same sex (due to the gender-segregated nature of prison confinement). As such, a host of issues regarding sexual orientation and gender roles are associated with the topic. In U.S. male prisons, rapists generally identify themselves as heterosexual and confine themselves to non-receptive sexual acts. Victims, commonly referred to as "punks" or "bitches", may or may not be seen as homosexual. "Punks" is a term for those who are generally confined to performing receptive sexual acts. Moreover, though "punks" are coerced into a sexual arrangement with an aggressor in exchange for protection, these men generally consider themselves heterosexual.

According to Algerian militant Abu Bacir El Assimi, Islamic terrorists rape young men as a means of recruitment for suicide bombings. Rape creates a social stigma and fear, according to reports, that leave Muslims prepared to die. "The sexual act on young recruits aged between 16 to 19 was a means to urge them to commit suicide operations."

Both rape and homosexual acts under Sharia law are punishable by death.

In one of the news report according News sources say an autopsy revealed a suspected terrorist bomber killed during an attempted terrorist attack on a security installation in Algeria may have been raped. The report presents the autopsy as finding: "a large tear in the anus of the terrorist, which confirms the sexual abuse." The victim of the alleged abuse was 22 years old who was said to have joined a terrorist group in March 2008.

If reports are true about sexual coercion of males or male rape being used to recruit young men to die in acts of terrorism, the concerns about how men are treated after male rape indicates the level of shame and indignities suffered. It was reported in Dubai in 2007 a very young French boy, Alex, age 15, who was kidnapped and sexually assaulted.

Sexual exploitation in corridor of power; Talking about political hierarchy: The notorious kingpins who inflict their dubious "leadership" on nations are often

Muammar Gaddafi could well be described as Sex Terrorist, "BBC documentary has eyewitness accounts of murder, torture and sexual abuse by the Libyan dictator, who was shot by rebels in 2011. Ousted Libyan dictator Muammar Gaddafi kidnapped and raped hundreds of teenagers in specially built sex dungeons, according to a **television documentary that was screened by BBC. The program titled, "Storyville: Mad Dog – Gaddafi's Secret World,"** Victims and witnesses state in the documentary that Gaddafi would choose his targets on visits to schools or colleges, patting on the head those who caught his eye.

Gaddafi security officials would then take the victim to one of several specially designed suites of rooms, where they would be abused and raped by the dictator. In one such suite at Tripoli University, there was found to be a fully-equipped gynaecological examination room, where victims were tested for sexually transmitted diseases before being sexually abused.

"Some of the girls were only 14 years old," recalled one teacher at a Tripoli school. "They would simply take the girl they wanted. They had no conscience, no morals, not an iota of mercy, even though she was a mere child." Some of the girls were held for years, while others were dumped with appalling injuries. Some victims were drafted into Gaddafi's unit of private female bodyguards, enduring years of rape and abuse and forced to witness the execution of opponents to the regime.

"The women would first be raped by the dictator then passed on, like used objects, to one of his sons and eventually to high-ranking officials for more sexual abuse," said Benghazi-based psychologist Seham Sergewa, who interviewed victims for the International Criminal Court.

Boys were also forced to serve in Gaddafi's harem. "He was terribly sexually deviant," recalled former chief of protocol Nuri Al Mismari. "Young boys and so on. He had his own boys. They used to be called the 'services group'."……

Once Gaddafi invited 20 young Italian models on a two-week all-expenses paid trip to Libya. A junket, if you will. The models (and by models, I mean prostitutes) later said that Gaddafi treated them like queens, but all denied the existence of the actual sex parties. (Or "bunga bunga" parties, in the parlance of our times).

Monstrous former Libyan dictator Gaddafi's death was as horrendous same as much the horror he committed in his life time. He was dragged from a drainpipe and shot by rebels in 2011, during Libya's civil war.

Former Iraqi dictator Saddam Hussein had two bloodthirsty sons who were just as crazy as he was – Uday and Qusay. Out of the entire terrible trio, Uday is thought to be the worst, an unforgiving psychopath who delighted only in sadism and cruelty. Until the US-led invasion of Iraq in 2003, little was known about the day-to-day lives of Uday and Qusay Hussein. But once Iraqis began to talk to the media, a seemingly never-ending string of unimaginably grim, grotesque stories began to emerge.

Most infamous is the account (recreated in the film The Devil's Double, about Uday and one of his personal decoys) concerns a 14-year-old girl – the daughter of a former provincial governor – with whom Uday became infatuated after spotting her at a party. Uday's bodyguards at first tried to simply lure her up to meet with the boss man, but she refused. When she reappeared three days later, she had been raped, but also provided with a new dress, a new watch, and some money. Her father complained to Saddam, and then went public with the story, leading Uday to threaten to kill the governor unless he submitted both of his daughters (the other one was 12 at that time) to be his new 'girlfriends.' The governor complied.

But that's just one story. There are other anecdotes, many of them almost too hideous to recount. One story tells of Uday crashing a wedding and kidnapping and raping the bride, leading the groom to kill himself. Another bride was raped and burned with chemicals while still in her wedding dress. Uday reportedly was so jealous of his brother Qusay (thought to be Saddam's favoured son), he insisted that any women who slept with his brother had to be kidnapped and brought to him for rape and torture. Sometimes he would utilize bizarre or historical methods of torture that he found out about on the Internet. Use of an iron maiden was said to be among his favourites. Uday's less violent but still peculiar proclivities over the long years of his father's absolute rule also captured the world's attention in 2003. Five nights a week, he'd throw private parties at the posh Baghdad Boat Club, with a rotating crop of beautiful young women invited for drinking and dancing. Near the close of the party, the female guests would be lined up and Uday would choose his favourites to keep for the night. He apparently never slept with the same girl more than two or three times. (The parties were only five nights a week, as Uday took two nights a week off from girls. "Fasting," as he called it.)

An ill man who had been grievously injured in an attempt on his life in 1996, Uday tried all sorts of unconventional remedies to cure himself, including bringing in a new mother to breastfeed him. (He hoped that the vitamin-rich milk might help to cure him. Plus I think he probably just enjoyed it too.)

Sex terror is not something new, discrimination against women is as old as recorded history, despite several feminist movement the world over demanding more equal rights for women and gender equality, these feminist movement have not succeeded in achieving their objectives.

Patriarchal religions, which mould most of the cultures of the world, subordinate women and girls to men. Fundamentalist movements, whether Christian, Jewish, Hindu or Islamic, advocate the repression of women and girls' sexuality. Women and girls' interaction with men and boys is closely monitored and restricted and their bodies and hair covered in a way deemed to be modest. For example, under the influence of Islamic fundamentalism, women are required to wear full body coverings, such as chadors and burqas. Punishment for sexual misconduct can be severe, as in Iran, where women can be legally stoned to death. The other form of control and abuse of women's sexuality is exploitation, in which women and girls are used for men's sexual gratification or profit. Women and children are sexually exploited when they are subjected to incest, rape, sexual harassment, battering, bride trafficking, pornography, and prostitution.

The law should delineate and prohibit behaviour which is socially abhorrent, against odious character. Of course, forcing women to have sex is much easier when the ladies are not highly trained Killing machines. The women are typically characterized as prophets of doom.

Women and women rights groups constant laments about inequality, discrimination in getting jobs and promotions and of sexual harassment at home or at workplace on beaches and in parks.

Domination by men of women is found in the Ancient near East as far back as 3100 BCE, as are restrictions on a woman's reproductive capacity and exclusion from "the process of representing or the construction of history." With the appearance of the Hebrews, there is also "the exclusion of woman from the God-humanity covenant."

Famine, starvation and mass-migrations related to land-abandonment severely traumatised the originally peaceful and sex-positive inhabitants of those lands, inducing a distinct turning away from original Matrism towards patristic forms of behaviour. In medieval Europe, patriarchy was not absolute, as female Empresses (such as **Theodora**) and Matriarchs (such as Helena, the mother of **Constantine**) enjoyed privilege, political rule, and societal honour.

The strategic use of rape in war is not a new phenomenon but only recently has it begun to be documented, chiefly in the Democratic Republic of Congo, Colombia and Sudan.

Sexual violation of women erodes the fabric of a community in a way that few weapons can. Rape's damage can be devastating because of the strong communal reaction to the violation and pain stamped on entire families. The harm inflicted in such cases on a woman by a rapist is an attack on her family and culture, as in many societies women are viewed as repositories of a community's cultural and spiritual values.

Article in "**Stop Human Trafficking in Thailand,**" comments, "Human trafficking is an international problem on a growing scale that affects millions of people each day. Thailand is particularly notorious for its high volume of human trafficking. It is estimated that eight billion dollars were generated from human trafficking in the last year alone. The term "human trafficking" is used to describe the experience of people who are "trafficked," or transported, for the purpose of forced labor and/or sexual slavery. Usually those who find themselves in these horrific situations are vulnerable people who exist at the fringes of society. In Thailand, a portion of the victims are migrants from North Korea, China, Vietnam, and other neighboring countries. However, many victims are also Thai natives, and no matter what their country of origin, many victims are women and children.

What makes Thailand such a high risk country for human trafficking? Thailand is a transit nation for many individuals fleeing their native land. People pour into

Thailand seeking refuge from poverty in North Korea, China, Vietnam, Pakistan, Burma and more. Although these citizens are seeking a better life, they enter into a nightmare as they are targeted and coerced into labor servitude and sexual slavery. Internal conflicts also put those native to Thailand at risk. Women and children who live in poverty often feel forced to sell themselves into enslavement in order to survive. The victims are forced into labor or prostitution either within Thailand or they are trafficked to other nations to do so."...............

In modern history, rape was used in World War II by the Nazi's, Soviets, and by the Japanese (as was the case with *'Comfort Women'* and the infamous *Rape of Nanking*), and it was also used in Vietnam. The last decade has seen a growing number of civil conflicts around the world that directly target women and girls. The numbers of rapes and other forms of sexual abuse have reached alarming levels, thus constituting an epidemic of sexual violence as a form of warfare. Countries such as: Afghanistan, Bangladesh, Guatemala, India, Liberia, Pakistan, Sierra Leone, Uganda, Sudan and the Congo, to name only a few have used, or currently use, rape as a weapon in conflict. In both a modern and historical context it is clear that all armies use rape as a weapon.

From the systematic rape of women in Bosnia, to an estimated 200,000 women raped during the battle for Bangladeshi independence in 1971, to Japanese rapes during the 1937 occupation of Nanking - the past century offers too many examples. So what motivates armed forces, whether state-backed troops or irregular militia, to attack civilian women and children? Rape is often used in ethnic conflicts as a way for attackers to perpetuate their social control and redraw ethnic boundaries, "Women are seen as the reproducers and carers of the community." "Therefore if one group wants to control another they often do it by impregnating women of the other community because they see it as a way of destroying the opposing community."

Germany in the spring of 1945. Hitler's Nazi regime was on the brink of defeat in the catastrophic war it had launched six years earlier. After invading and occupying large swathes of Eastern Europe and the Soviet Union -- and murdering tens of millions of people in the process -- the German army was retreating, and the Red Army was following hot on its heels, intent on revenge.

One of the twentieth century's greatest crimes, and probably one of the greatest crimes against women in history, was the mass rape of the conquered women of Europe after the Judeo-Communist victory there in 1945. The rapists were mainly Soviet Union (Russian) Red Army soldiers, some of them non-White troops from the Far East and Central Asian Republics of the Soviet Union. They were brutes no doubt, but they were permitted and encouraged to indulge their lower than bestial urges by official "Allied" policies which incited hatred particularly against the Germans, but also against those of other European nationalities which were then allied with Germany in an anti-Communist bloc. One cannot contemplate this great mass orgy of rape, gang rape, and sexual slavery of innocent women and little girls without revulsion.

Sweeping across German territory, many of the Russian soldiers burned, killed, looted. And they also raped German women. The Soviets, of course, weren't the only ones, soldiers from other Allied armies were also guilty of sexual violence as they moved into Germany from the West. But most agree that the problem was particularly acute in eastern Germany. Historians estimate that close to 2 million German women and girls were raped in the closing months of the war, many women were repeatedly raped.

As the Red Army advanced towards her in 1945, the German city of Berlin had become a city virtually without men. Out of a civilian population of 2,700,000, 2,000,000 were women. It is small wonder that the fear of sexual attack raced through the city like a plague. Doctors were besieged by patients seeking information on the quickest way to commit suicide, and poison was in great demand. This ghastly crime perpetrated mainly by what US President Franklin Roosevelt called "our noble Soviet ally."

A wave of rapes and sexual violence occurred in Central Europe in 1944–45, as the Western Allies and the Red Army fought their way into the Third Reich. On the territory of the Nazi Germany, it began on 21 October 1944 when troops of the Red Army crossed the bridge over the Angerapp creek (marking the border) and committed the Nemmersdorf massacre before they were beaten back a few hours later.

The majority of the assaults were committed in the Soviet occupation zone, estimates of the numbers of German women raped by Soviet soldiers ranged up to 2 million. In many cases women were the victims of repeated rapes, some as many as 60 to 70 times. At least 100,000 women are believed to have been raped in **Berlin**, based on surging abortion rates in the following months and contemporary hospital reports, with an estimated 10,000 women dying in the aftermath. Female deaths in connection with the rapes in Germany, overall, are estimated at 240,000. **Antony Beevor** describes it as the "greatest phenomenon of mass **rape** in history", and has concluded that at least 1.4 million women were raped in East Prussia, Pomerania and Silesia alone.

Asian men of Mongolian origins and Central Asians were brought to Berlin including Black soldiers from U.S and France. Black soldiers from America and France over 10,000 in Germany and Berlin, some thousands of German white women were raped. There were hundreds to thousands of abandoned brown babies born from Black soldiers of African origin in Germany. Mongolian and Central Asian troops mostly in Berlin. Some German historians claim that 100,000 German white women rape were committed by Asian men of mostly Mongolian origin and including central Asian origin (Kazakh, Kyrgyz) many of those rape victim the white German women were hospitalized, killed or committed suicide.

Historian Norman Naimark writes that after the summer of 1945, Soviet soldiers caught raping civilians were usually punished to some degree, ranging from arrest to execution. However, the rapes continued until the winter of 1947–48, when Soviet occupation authorities finally confined Soviet troops to strictly guarded posts and camps, separating them from the residential population in the Soviet zone of Germany.

In December of 1937, the Japanese Imperial Army marched into China's capital city of Nanking and proceeded to murder 300,000 out of 600,000 civilians and soldiers in the city. The six weeks of carnage would become known as the Rape of

Nanking and represented the single worst atrocity during the World War II era in either the European or Pacific Theatres of War.

The elimination of the Chinese POWs began after they were transported by trucks to remote locations on the outskirts of Nanking. As soon as they were assembled, the savagery began, with young Japanese soldiers encouraged by their superiors to inflict maximum pain and suffering upon individual POWs as a way of toughening themselves up for future battles, and also to eradicate any civilized notions of mercy. Filmed footage and still photographs taken by the Japanese themselves document the brutality. Smiling soldiers can be seen conducting bayonet practice on live prisoners, decapitating them and displaying severed heads as souvenirs, and proudly standing among mutilated corpses. Some of the Chinese POWs were simply mowed down by machine-gun fire while others were tied-up, soaked with gasoline and burned alive.

After the destruction of the POWs, the soldiers turned their attention to the women of Nanking and an outright animalistic hunt ensued. Old women over the age of 70 as well as little girls under the age of 8 were dragged off to be sexually abused. More than 20,000 females (with some estimates as high as 80,000) were gang-raped by Japanese soldiers, then stabbed to death with bayonets or shot so they could never bear witness. Pregnant women were not spared. In several instances, they were raped, then had their bellies slit open and the foetuses torn out. Sometimes, after storming into a house and encountering a whole family, the Japanese forced Chinese men to rape their own daughters, sons to rape their mothers, and brothers their sisters, while the rest of the family was made to watch.

The phrase "comfort women" is a controversial term that refers to approximately 200,000 women who were recruited as prostitutes by the Imperial Japanese Army during World War II. Many of the young women were forced into servitude and exploited as sex slaves throughout Asia, becoming victims of the largest case of human trafficking in the 20th century. The trade of comfort women is thus a massive violation of human rights that's been left out of our textbooks, leaving the individuals embroiled in the atrocious practice to be remembered merely as abstract characters in a taboo history.

'Comfort woman' is a translation of the Japanese euphemism, Jugun Janfu, The first comfort station was established in the Japanese concession in Shanghai in 1932. Earlier comfort women were Japanese prostitutes who volunteered for such service. However, as Japan continued military expansion, the military found itself short of Japanese volunteers, and turned to the local population to coerce women into serving in these stations. Many women responded to calls for work as factory workers or nurses, and did not know that they were being pressed into sexual slavery. The military turned to acquiring comfort women outside mainland Japan, especially from Korea and occupied China. Many women were tricked or defrauded into joining the military brothel. When the locals, especially Chinese, were considered hostile, Japanese soldiers carried out the "Three All's Policy" which included indiscriminately kidnapping and raping local civilians.

In Europe, **German military brothels** were set up by the **Third Reich** (**Nazi Germany** and the **Third Reich** are common names for Germans during the period from 1933 to 1945, when its government was controlled by Adolf Hitler and his National Socialist German Workers' Party (NSDAP), commonly known as the Nazi Party) during World-war 2 throughout much of occupied Europe for the use of **Wehrmacht** and Schutz-Staffel soldiers. These brothels were generally new creations but in the West they were sometimes set up using existing brothels. Until 1942, there were around 500 military brothels of this kind in Nazi occupied Europe. Often operating in confiscated hotels and guarded by the **Wehrmacht**, these facilities used to serve travelling soldiers and those withdrawn from the front. It is estimated that, along with those in **concentration camp brothels**, at least 34,140 European women were forced to serve as prostitutes during the German occupation. In many cases in Eastern Europe, the women involved were kidnapped on the streets of occupied cities during German military and police round ups.

In an attempt to shine light on this oft-forgotten segment of WWII history," "Most were teenagers... and were raped by between 10 to 100 soldiers a day at military rape camps," "Women were starved, beaten, tortured, and killed. By some estimates only 25 to 30 percent survived the ordeal." Human trafficking is the fastest growing industry in the world, and the second largest business after arms dealing in the 21st century. So, the comfort women issue is not just about the past, but it is very relevant even today.

In modern era, in 21st century we have read about and have seen images of extreme wildest of inhuman activity, particularly so in most of the Muslim dominated countries in west-Asia and in North-Africa. The brutal and venomous Sunni-Muslim jihadist terrorist groups such as BOKO-Haram and Al-Shabaab and most severe and brutal jihadist group of all the "ISIS (Islamic State of Iraq & al-Sham)" these ferocious jihadist (Islamic Holy-warrior) groups staunchly believes in enslaving young women and girls and sexually exploiting them, however we should find out few details about past history as well of hatred crimes and slavery, here what reminds me is the history of brutal atrocities that was so remorselessly unleashed on Irish white-women; **Article title "The Irish Slave Trade – The Forgotten "White Slaves"** describes the most ugliest form of discrimination of Irish women; *"They came as slaves; vast human cargo transported on tall British ships bound for the Americas. They were shipped by the hundreds of thousands and included men, women, and even the youngest of children.*

Whenever they rebelled or even disobeyed an order, they were punished in the harshest ways. Slave owners would hang their human property by their hands and set their hands or feet on fire as one form of punishment. They were burned alive and had their heads placed on pikes in the marketplace as a warning to other captives.
We don't really need to go through all of the gory details, do we? We know all too well the atrocities of the African slave trade.
But, are we talking about African slavery? King James II and Charles I also led a continued effort to enslave the Irish. Britain's famed Oliver Cromwell furthered this practice of dehumanizing one's next door neighbour.

The Irish slave trade began when James II sold 30,000 Irish prisoners as slaves to the New World. His Proclamation of 1625 required Irish political prisoners be sent overseas and sold to English settlers in the West Indies. By the mid 1600s, the Irish were the main slaves sold to Antigua and Montserrat. At that time, 70% of the total population of Montserrat were Irish slaves.

Ireland quickly became the biggest source of human livestock for English merchants. The majority of the early slaves to the New World were actually white.

From 1641 to 1652, over 500,000 Irish were killed by the English and another 300,000 were sold as slaves. Ireland's population fell from about 1,500,000 to 600,000 in one single decade. Families were ripped apart as the British did not allow Irish dads to take their wives and children with them across the Atlantic.

This led to a helpless population of homeless women and children. Britain's solution was to auction them off as well. During the 1650s, over 100,000 Irish children between the ages of 10 and 14 were taken from their parents and sold as slaves in the West Indies, Virginia and New England. In this decade, 52,000 Irish (mostly women and children) were sold to Barbados and Virginia. Another 30,000 Irish men and women were also transported and sold to the highest bidder. In 1656, Cromwell ordered that 2000 Irish children be taken to Jamaica and sold as slaves to English settlers.

Many people today will avoid calling the Irish slaves what they truly were: Slaves. They'll come up with terms like "Indentured Servants" to describe what occurred to the Irish. However, in most cases from the 17th and 18th centuries, Irish slaves were nothing more than human cattle.

As an example, the African slave trade was just beginning during this same period. It is well recorded that African slaves, not tainted with the stain of the hated Catholic theology and more expensive to purchase, were often treated far better than their Irish counterparts."...., so this is a brief summary of how humans have been discriminated all across the demographics throughout the world since generations."................

I want y'all to imagine an orgy of rape like this happening in your country, in your neighbourhood, to your family, to your wife, your sister, your daughter. I want you to imagine what it would feel like to be totally powerless to stop it from happening, completely unable to bring the criminals to justice.

Journalists and human rights organization have documented campaigns of genocidal rape during the conflicts in the Balkans, **Sierra-Leone**, Rwanda, Liberia, Sudan, Uganda, and the **Democratic Republic of Congo**. The strategic aim of these mass rapes are twofold. The first is to instil terror in the civilian population, with the intent to forcibly dislocate them from their property. The second is to degrade the chance of possible return and reconstitution by inflicting humiliation and shame on the targeted population. These effects are strategically important for non-state actors, as it is necessary for them to remove the targeted population from the land. The use of mass rape is well suited for campaigns which involve ethnic cleansing and genocide, as the objective is to destroy or forcefully remove the target population, and ensure they do not return.

It is estimated that nearly six million people have died in the **Democratic Republic of Congo** since 1996 as a result of conflict and conflict related causes (as much as 90% due to malaria, diarrhea, pneumonia and malnutrition, aggravated by displaced population living in unsanitary and over-crowded conditioned that lacked access to shelter, water, food and medicine), nearly 50 percent of them children under the age of Five. Forty-five thousand continue to die each month.

Hundreds of thousands of women have been raped as a weapon of war. One study estimates that as many as 400,000 women may be raped there each year. Additionally, sexual assault is visited on men and children at an incomprehensible level, all of which serves to destabilize, divide and destroy the spirit of the people.

In some raids in Rwanda, virtually every adolescent girl who survived an attack by the militia was subsequently raped. Many of those who became pregnant were ostracized by their families and communities. Some abandoned their babies, while others committed suicide.

War and civil unrest also contribute to increase violence in the home, according to recent studies. Death, upheaval and poverty increase tensions within the family and the likelihood of violence against girls and women. Men who feel that they have lost the ability to protect their women may compensate by exercising violent control over them at home.

The beginning of the end of the use of rape as a weapon of war is to combat gender inequalities and stereotypes in cultures while in peace time, as a method to prevent and curb the use of rape as a weapon of war. Removing the stigma of rape is the first and foremost crucial step to see that the ripple effects do not continue to haunt our global society in future generations and centuries.

Representatives of the 200,000 "comfort women" forcibly drafted into military sexual slavery by Japan from 1928 until the end of World War II are still fighting for restitution. Far from colluding, women from Korea, China, Taiwan, the Philippines, Malaysia and East Timor were "severely coerced" into prostitution.

The tolerance and standardization of rape as a weapon of war is what has led to its impunity at an international scale, and thus increased its silence. Impunity regarding the increasingly brutalization of the use of rape as a weapon of war, combined with its effectiveness, only provokes its use. The reason for such is that the perpetrators are less likely to be tried and punished for the use of this weapon during times of armed conflict than any other weapon, and if convictions do follow the punishment is disproportionate to the crime.

With the world waking up to how serious the issue of rape is, governments need to ensure severe sanctions are in place to ensure that rape is not used as a weapon of war. It is time to punish states that use rape as an unlawful weapon in armed conflict.

The failure to treat war rape like other illegal weapons or war tactics removes the central protection of the laws governing the conduct of war from rape victims, mainly women and girls. Victims' rights to accountability and reparations for their injuries from the use of illegal weapons is separate and in addition to their rights to accountability for other crimes arising out of the same act, including having perpetrators charged with rape as a war crime, a crime against humanity or a constituent element of genocide.

The emergence of HIV/AIDS in the past two decades, and the complex interaction between the virus and conflicts, has reinforced both the human and state security dimensions of disease. Whilst the state security dimension focuses on the collapse of the apparatus of governance, the human security dimension focuses on threats to the vulnerable groups, especially women and girls, during conflicts.

Although the history of wars and conflicts is replete with massive and systematic sexual violence against vulnerable women, modern-day wars in African nations and elsewhere are increasingly characterized by the use of rape as a weapon of war, the intentional or wilful transmission of the HIV to innocent victims, and the neglect of these victims in post-conflict reconstruction programmes. The magnitude of sexual violence in conflict situations will never be fully known, since the stigma associated with being a victim discourages women and girls from reporting the crime.

Ethiopia is estimated to have one of the highest rates of violence against women in the world. A report by the UN found that nearly 60% of Ethiopian women were subjected to sexual violence. Rape is a very serious problem in Ethiopia. The country is infamous for the practice of marriage by abduction, with the prevalence of this practice in Ethiopia being one of the highest in the world. In many parts of Ethiopia, it is common for a man, working in co-ordination with his friends, to kidnap a girl or woman, sometimes using a horse to ease the escape. The abductor will then hide his intended bride and rape her until she becomes pregnant. Girls as young as eleven years old are reported to have been kidnapped for the purpose of marriage. Also the Ethiopian military has been accused of committing systematic rapes against civilians.

It goes without saying that India struggles to deal with the issue of rape, so much so, every 20 minutes, someone in **India is raped**. The problem of patriarchy couldn't be more salient right now. Some perspective is needed here. Not every man in India echoes anywhere near as brutal, disrespectful and sexist views towards rape. A lot of men, women and even children are fed up with the frequency of rape in India, Rape is too commonplace in India. It's too much of "ah' oh" she got raped last night? Probably was her fault' type of sickening attitude that is deeply instilled into Indian culture, and it would seem, people of India have had enough. Some men in India view women as no more than a compilation of breasts, a vagina and facial features who if they act "out of line," get sanctioned, as if Indian women are an Indian man's pet.

One explanation could stem from the perception that even if a women is raped, she won't speak up to report it, as sexual assault is perceived as a source of shame in India. The rape itself is one thing, but given how judgemental and cynical Indians can often be, it must be tough for a women to admit she has been raped, considering most Indian's consider rape to be worse than death, likening a raped women to a walking corpse. What a painfully hopeless situation. The problem of rape is rooted in the power in India a lot of the time, less so in sexual motive. A women is often raped to remind her, not to over-step cultural boundaries, and if you do, well you should expect to get raped.

It's no surprise that India has been ranked as one of the worst countries for women by The Reuters Trust Law group. According to the 2012 UNICEF report, about 53% of Indian girls and 57% of Indian boys between the age group of 15 – 19, think that beating a wife is normal and justified. Also, as per a national family health survey, a sizeable percent of women blame themselves for getting bashings from their husbands.

Women in India are not safe outside their homes and some don't feel secure at home as well. Indian authorities blatantly admit that the country's public places are unsafe for women. According to a report by Women and Child Development Ministry, most of the Indian streets are poorly lit and there's also a lack of women's toilets, making it highly unsafe for women to travel around, especially during the night. Women who fag or booze are widely considered as morally loose in the Indian society and according to the village councils, women talking on cell phones and going to the local markets are responsible for increasing rape incidents.

In Western media's sporadic and reductive coverage, the idea that India is a country plagued by rampant, "extreme" sexual violence becomes an all-too-familiar trope. This focus on "rampant" and "extreme" simultaneously manages to overstate and understate sexual violence in India. On the one hand, the Western media alleges that India has a "cultural problem" when it comes to violence against women; on the other, it refuses to take notice of rapes and sexual violence, let alone sexual harassment, that are not "extreme" enough to make headlines.

The rapes of women in the country aroused the deliberation of Indian society's beliefs which, as depicted in various Indian cultures and literature, treats women as goddesses and men as protectors of women. The rape incidents prompted scrutiny of the degrading treatment of women internally in the country and externally spread an abhorrent impression around the world.

The idea that a man is predatory and dangerous by nature is so, so harmful to both men and women. You know the whole school dress code debate and how it's skewed against girls thanks to issues like rape culture and slut shaming? It's saying that girls are responsible for "distracting boys" if they dress a certain way that adults find unacceptable, but it's *also* saying that boys are highly distractable and can't control themselves. Saying "boys will be boys" makes everyone helpless: it teaches boys they're not responsible for their own impulses, even (especially) if they're violent and/or sexual.

Why does society not teach men not to rape? Even if a woman is as this British actress describes, drunk, fashionably mini-skirted and staggering about, should human decency not cause a man to make sure she gets home safely without attacking her and violating her. Does she not have the right to dress however she pleases, or however pleases her? They should be taught from kindergarten to university and beyond not to rape. Just like they're taught their ABCs and not to steal and they should learn the lessons and never forget them. In fact, they should be made scared to rape.

We know it's not *all* men, but its men. That is a stone hard, iron cast, indelible, inescapable, global fact. And when women try to talk to men about rape, look how they behave. Even the good ones manage to sound like total uneducable tossers. 'Get a sense of humour?"

Are these men imprisoned by lust and greed or are they truly living every man's fantasy? Talking about the enslavement and deprivation that the sex tourists create for themselves. This made me wonder, what if **we rescued men from false ideas** (e.g. conquering heroes deserve the fawning of many women, sexual conquest means men are sexy and wanted, sex with virgins leads to purity, multiple sexual partners of multiple ages, ethnicities multiple times prove they are really Men's Men) **as proactively and passionately as we rescued their victims from human trafficking.**

If you were raised in a society of humans, you possess a basic moral code not to cause harm to others. This includes rape, whereby a man has sex with a woman who rather not have sex with him at that moment in time. But let's say you're a feral man who was raised by wolves. You enter society with the belief that it's quite normal to force yourself upon a woman.

Human trafficking is the second largest form of organized crime in the world. It is essentially the "buying and selling of human beings". The U.N estimates that about 2.5 million people from 127 countries are trafficked around the world, every year. Nearly every country is a source, transit or destination (or combination of these three) for trafficked victims.

Human trafficking occurs in a various industries including: agriculture, hospitality, and sweatshops However, about 80% of human trafficking cases reported are related to sex slavery and sexual exploitation. This is referred to as "sex trafficking".

There are some 50,000 people a year who are sold and end up in slavery-like conditions in the United States, and that's on farms, in factories, in private homes, in brothels and in the sex industry. They come from all over the world, and it's based on economic hardship. Women are lured from their home countries and children are pushed out by their families because of the extreme economic conditions that they face.

Rape culture is what happens when survivors of rape are blamed for provoking an attack, for not being "smart" enough about their choices, or for otherwise being responsible for their rape.

According to report prepared by "AIHRC: 400 rape, honour killings registered in Afghanistan," "Around four hundred cases of rape and honour-killing have been filed with the Afghanistan Independent Human Rights Commission (AIHRC) during the past two years. AIHRC officials called the latest statistics as "shocking" and expressed concerns that majority of similar cases have not been recorded due to strict traditional sensitivities. Head of the Afghanistan Independent Human Rights Commission (AIHRC) Seema Samar said legal, political, traditional, social, economic and psychological issues are the main motives behind growing violence across the country.

Suraya Sobhrang, head of the women's' affairs department in Afghanistan Independent Human Rights Commission said around 240 cases of honor-killing and 160 cases of rape have been recorded across the country last year.

Ms. Sobhrang said the statistic does not include overall violence cases across the country and majority of them are hidden by victim's families.

According to AIHRC findings around 21 percent of honor-killings were committed by husbands of the victims, 7 percent of the honor killing were done by brothers of victims, 4 percent by fathers, while brother of the husband, mother and other relatives forms the remaining percentage of 57 percent who committed honor killings across the country. While the remaining 43 percent of those who were involved behind the honor killing remains unknown.

In the meantime AIHRC said that the latest finding shows that 65 percent of the rape cases were committed by unknown individuals, while close relatives were involved in 35 percent of rape cases which includes 4 percent by fathers, 2 percent by brothers, 1 percent by uncles and 10 percent by neighbors of the victims. The findings also shows that 15 percent of honor killing and rape were committed by Afghan police officers. AIHRC also stated that judiciary institutions blame rape victims for the crime and convict them for punishment."............

Article title "**Human Trafficking Facts / Sex Slavery and ... > Soroptimist**" describes about sex trafficking; "Sex trafficking or slavery is the exploitation of women and children, within national or across international borders, for the purposes of forced sex work. Commercial sexual exploitation includes pornography, prostitution and sex trafficking of women and girls, and is characterized by the exploitation of a human being in exchange for goods or money. Each year, an estimated 800,000 women and children are trafficked across international borders—though additional numbers of women and girls are trafficked within countries.

Some sex trafficking is highly visible, such as street prostitution. But many trafficking victims remain unseen, operating out of unmarked brothels in unsuspecting—and sometimes suburban—neighborhoods. Sex traffickers may also operate out of a variety of public and private locations, such as massage parlors, spas and strip clubs.

Adult women make up the largest group of sex trafficking victims, followed by girl children, although a small percentage of men and boys are trafficked into the sex industry as well.

Human trafficking migration patterns tend to flow from East to West, but women may be trafficked from any country to another country at any given time and trafficking victims exist everywhere. Many of the poorest and most unstable countries have the highest incidences of human trafficking, and extreme poverty is a common bond among trafficking victims. Where economic alternatives do not exist, women and girls are more vulnerable to being tricked and coerced into sexual servitude. Increased unemployment and the loss of job security have undermined women's incomes and economic position. A stalled gender wage gap, as well as an increase in women's part-time and informal sector work, push women into poorly-paid jobs and long-term and hidden unemployment, which leaves women vulnerable to sex traffickers."................

Article title **"Sex Trafficking / Fight Slavery Now**:" writes; "A major proportion of Human Trafficking is for sexual purposes, with the victims overwhelmingly women and young girls. According to one frequently cited study, **the *average* age of entry into prostitution in the U.S. among prostituted minors, is just thirteen!** An overwhelming majority of these children have been victims of sexual abuse and violence preceding their commercial exploitation. This shocking fact belies the notion that prostitution is a reasonable choice made rationally by a woman of her own free will.

Often called "sexual slavery", this may include not only prostitution, but also other roles in the 'sexploitation' industry such as massage parlors, fetish clubs, strip clubs, phone sex operations, exotic dancing establishments, the production of pornography for the photo, video, and film markets, and even the marketing of child 'brides'. In all of these instances victims are often coerced, cajoled, threatened, tricked, or simply forced... and end up in a situation where they are no longer in control. In 2006 the FBI estimated that 100,000 children and young women were trafficked for sexual purposes within the US, and that the majority of them were not runaways but people coerced by predators.

The manner in which women are initially induced and finally forced to resign themselves to being used by others, is a rigorously time tested method that relies on a host of techniques for breaking people. This is coldly known as the 'seasoning process'. It may involve any combination of humiliation, privation, isolation, and violence or the threat of it, both to the victim and to her family.

The Coalition Against Trafficking in Women calls prostitution "the world's oldest *oppression*!" and proposes that all forms of prostitution are necessarily exploitative. Some have suggested that prostitution is tantamount to 'pay to rape'. While other views may differ, no one denies the clear connection between sex trafficking and prostitution."......................

In the context of social work, it is important for practitioners to be knowledgeable about global sex trafficking from both micro and macro practice perspectives. Since the social work profession is committed to poverty reduction, empowering vulnerable populations, and eliminating gender-based oppression, it is imperative to recognize that human trafficking and the international sex trade encompass issues that violate the principles of social justice and human dignity.

For decades, conservatives have claimed that women can't get pregnant from "legitimate" rape thanks to their wise, all-knowing uteri, psychic "juices" and Spidey Sense-like "secretions."

It has been argued that fear promotes ovulation, and that women who are raped have a ten-per-cent risk of pregnancy; there are estimates of as little as one per cent. Numbers are also skewed when they are adjusted to include or exclude women not of reproductive age; for sodomy and other forms of rape that cannot cause pregnancy; for rape victims who may be using oral birth control or I.U.D.s; and for women who are raped and become or are pregnant as a result of consensual sex with a husband or partner who is not the rapist, before or after the rape.

Women who are being abused on an ongoing basis are particularly likely to conceive in rape. Catherine MacKinnon has written, "Forced pregnancy is familiar, beginning in rape and proceeding through the denial of abortions; this occurred during slavery and still happens to women who cannot afford abortions."

Historically, rape has been seen less as a violation of a woman than as a theft from a man to whom that woman belonged, either her husband or her father, who suffered an economic loss (a woman's marriageability spoiled) and an insult to his honour.

Rape culture is used to encapsulate any actions or representations of sexual violence that is scarily treated as the norm or expected of society. It was **first coined** by feminist groups in the 1970s, appalled by the lack of sensitivity when discussing or treating rape victims (a majority of them being girls and women) and the media's obsession with graphic, sexual imagery.

The aftermath of rape is always complicated. Many victims are simply in denial that they are pregnant in the first place: a full third of the pregnancies resulting from rape are not discovered until the second trimester. Any delay in detection reduces women's options, especially outside major urban centres, but many women struggle with the speed of the decision; they are still recovering from being raped when they are called on to make up their minds about an abortion. The decision of whether or not to carry through with such a pregnancy is nearly always an ordeal that can lead, no matter which choice is ultimately made, to depression, anxiety, insomnia, and P.T.S.D. Rape is a permanent damage; it leaves not scars, but open wounds. As one woman said, "You can abort the child, but not the experience."

Finally, factor in what is certainly one of the most important reasons why a rape victim rarely gets pregnant, and that's physical trauma. Every woman is aware that stress and emotional factors can alter her menstrual cycle. To get and stay pregnant a woman's body must produce a very sophisticated mix of hormones. Hormone production is controlled by a part of the brain that is easily influenced by emotions. There's no greater emotional trauma that can be experienced by a woman than an assault rape. This can radically upset her possibility of ovulation, fertilization, implantation and even nurturing of a pregnancy. So what further percentage reduction in pregnancy will this cause? No one knows, but this factor certainly cuts this last figure by at least 50 percent and probably more.

Simple rape" is defined as someone having sex with another person without their consent. Rape is ultimately the rapist's fault, *not* the victim's. if you are raped, it is 100% the rapist's fault, and that nothing you did, wore, or said could have caused you to be raped. There is no such thing as "asking for it," and anyone who leads you to believe otherwise is deeply misguided.

If we work, as a society, to raise men who are respectful of women and stop contributing to a culture that objectifies and belittles women constantly, then we can slowly start to turn things around. Sometimes, adolescent boys think "rape jokes" are funny and that it's okay to joke around about sexual assault, and it's important to let them know that this is not the case. Men can also be raped, but society has taken into itself that men "can't possibly be raped", and so most men are ashamed and afraid if they speak out. We intend to empower women by giving them some sensible advice on how to avoid danger. However, **women are not the only sex to be raped. Men can be raped, but it just isn't as prevalent. Society doesn't believe "petite little women" can rape "big strong men", and yet it still happens.** When you're in a social situation with someone you know, be extra careful and don't fully let your guard down unless you feel truly safe with the person. Even then, rape can occur. Always be alert and if your gut tells you the situation is not okay, you should leave as soon and as safely as you can.

Everyone is in search of the cause of child rape but no one is finding ways to prevent this dreadful act from happening. Many of the morning T.V shows have interviewed the culprits but what is actually the use of all this? Mostly the people who commit this dreadful crime are often frivolous and less concern about social affair and they usually do not watch morning shows then how are we planning to teach them a lesson?

Perpetrators of Child sexual abuse isn't always easy to spot since there is no mark or visible sign written on someone's face that he or she is a rapist or an abuser of young children, but its predisposing factors most definitely can be reduced. We are tired of these reports, of children being wickedly lured into the arms of some obviously mentally deranged human for sexual gratification.

Increasing Awareness is to educate your daughters about rape as soon as possible. This extremely increasing news about child rape shows that this has now become a sort of a global trend. I am sorry to say this, but humanity is decreasing day by day and there is no difference between animals and people who commit this crime. It is so disturbing and depressing that in this era most cases of rape involve little girls whose age is in between 6 to 12 years. Every one of us has daughter and sisters and if not then we do have mothers. Can we see them in the place of these little angels? The answer is never. However, one cannot control the other but as parents one should guide their children about this seriously devastating social ill. The children usually consider weird and scary looking people as strangers and they do not talk to them but they must be told that not every stranger is wicked looking. These days behind the angelic faces demons are present. I would suggest each and every parents to please not to leave your child in care of stranger and even that of suspicious relatives and friends, make your child understand that talking to any stranger will harm them. In case where they feel that some stranger is approaching them, or even a known person is behaving strangely and making explicit overtures they should call for help immediately.

If you've experienced sexual abuse by a family member you are not alone — and what happened to you is not your fault. While it may be difficult to talk about, you should know that this is an issue that impacts many people. In fact, over 1/3 of perpetrators in cases of child sexual abuse are family members. It can be difficult for an individual to disclose sexual assault or abuse when they know the perpetrator. It can be especially difficult if the perpetrator is a family member.

To understand more about child sex abuse, Article title "**Types of Sexual Violence / Child Sexual Abuse**" writes; "Child sexual abuse is a form of child abuse that includes sexual activity with a minor. A child cannot consent to any form of sexual activity, period. When a perpetrator engages with a child this way, they are committing a crime that can have lasting effects on the victim for years.

The majority of perpetrators are someone the child or family knows. As many as **93% of victims under the age of 18 know the abuser.** A perpetrator does not have to be an adult to harm a child. They can have any relationship to the child including an older sibling or playmate, family member, a teacher, a coach or instructor, a caretaker, or the parent of another child. According to **1 in 6,** "[Child] sexual abuse is the result of abusive behaviour that takes advantage of a child's vulnerability and is in no way related to the sexual orientation of the abusive person."

Abusers can manipulate victims to stay quiet about the sexual abuse using a number of different tactics. Often an abuser will use their position of power over the victim to coerce or intimidate the child. They might tell the child that the activity is normal or that they enjoyed it. An abuser may make threats if the child refuses to participate or plans to tell another adult. Child sexual abuse is not only a physical violation; it is a violation of trust and/or authority."............

First of all the parents should keep a watch on the daily activities of their children just by befriending with them and spending some time with them on regular basis without giving an impression that spending time with them is only to elicit information from them to use against them later. Break the barrier and let them know about the body parts and educate them about good touch and bad touch. Talk to them about sex not like a parent but as a senior friend with experience who guides a junior. Let them talk about the unusual behaviour found in outsiders. Do not scare them in advance but let them come out with their observations by prompting but not by suggesting. Children should be taught to remember their names, parents' details, address, contact numbers of parents and also helpline numbers to use in case of emergency. A child abuse is a threat to the nation. The chances of intellectual growth of a child may get hampered due to no mistake of the child or parents but because of a third person which ultimately hampers national growth.

Article "**Teens who blame rape victims**" has written, "**Teenagers are less likely to be sympathetic to sex attack survivors,** who had been drinking or flirting before they were attacked than people in their 20s, 30s and 40s.

According to research from the **Office for National Statistics,** 34 per cent of 16 to 19 years old believed a victim's drunkenness made them "completely", "mostly" or "a little" responsible for the assault, along with nearly 46 per cent who said the same about a victim who had been flirting with their attacker.
In comparison, only 34 per cent of adults aged 45 to 54 thought a victim was responsible for the attack if they'd flirted heavily beforehand.

It is a worrying result and one which Sarah Green, director of the End Violence Against Women Coalition, blames on a confused sexualized culture.

"Young people today are bombarded with confusing and conflicting messages about men and women and sexuality in popular culture – women are constantly portrayed as sex objects and it is implied that it is 'natural' for men to pursue women to the point of coercion," she said.

"We already know that a significant minority of the population are inclined to blame women for being raped, but what should be a cause of great concern in these figures is the fact that younger people are significantly more likely to blame women and girls for rape."..............

Just a few years ago, sexual abuse wasn't really a topic of conversation. Victims of assault often felt isolated, unrepresented, and ultimately hopeless. It's true that lots of crimes still don't get reported. But the world's on an upward trend towards bringing attackers to justice and really starting to talk openly about the problem. However, discussion of sexual assault is still highly controversial. And part of that controversy stems from the way gender roles interact are tied to the conversation about rape. One thing that's easily lost in the mire is the fact that rape can happen to anyone — male or female. Rape is also about establishing power, not sexual attraction, and many people forget that distinction.

Sexual violence is devastating to all victims, regardless of gender, and many reactions are shared by both male and female victims. You may feel rage, shame, guilt, powerlessness, helplessness, concern regarding your safety, and/or symptoms of physical illness. You need to know that strong or weak; outgoing or withdrawn; gay, straight, or bisexual; old or young; whatever your physical appearance, you have done nothing that justifies this violence against you. At no point and under no circumstances does anyone have the right to violate or control another. Sexually violent crimes are often embedded in issues of violence and power, not of lust or passion. Feeling responsible is a normal reaction to sexual violence. However, sexual violence is never the responsibility of the survivor; you did nothing to deserve this.

Our cultural norms tend to silence those men arguably more than they do women. Popular culture says men should be stoic, silent, and unemotional; it's far from supportive of the emotions and aftermath of sexual assault for men. In fact, young men are given a pat on the back for acquiring sexual experience (even if it's with a woman much older than appropriate for his age) without much emotional support.

Male survivors of rape can be left with concerns about their sexual orientation, or shame because they became unwillingly aroused during the incident. Sometimes, they'll feel fear that the assault could change their original orientation. Because of certain beliefs that are ingrained in our social climate, victims may feel emasculated by sexual assault and angry that they weren't "strong enough" to fight off their attacker. Anyone who's survived an assault, male or female, young or old, deserves support to cope with the devastating emotional consequences. But male survivors might believe they aren't worthy of asking for help, because they feel they weren't "man" enough to stop the abuse, or in some cases may not even ask for help because they're too ashamed. Those fears are rooted in reality. That shame comes directly from a dangerous cultural belief that **sexual violence doesn't affect men**. But the truth is, it does. And ignoring it definitely won't make it go away. The world can make a difference for male victims of rape. By beginning to pay attention to the truth, we'll start to pave the road to change.

The purpose of laws is to guide and streamline the society within the limits guided by moral judgment and to guard against the miscreants and criminals. This may work sometimes, but in most cases, laws have failed or have the loopholes for others to take advantage to frame others of crime for their own vested interests. The laws can be faulty in dispensing justice which is either based on the principle of revenge in most cases, circling those involved who are handed over the verdict, sometimes wrongfully with no recourse for the accused to counter the judgment. The laws are ever being evolved to make them better and well suited for the sufferers, but it can never be perfect, for the fault lines are much graver when it comes to punishment, and the punishment bestowed with a lack of evidence is hellish.

Domestic violence is a bigger menace than compare to terrorism or conventional military wars, yes, surprising, but this is what many research surveys and studies conducted by many human rights and civil rights groups have found out that domestic violence is much more devastatingly harmful, troublesome and cost-wise as well very expensive than compare to terrorism or wars fought by military in the battlefields.

The menace of Domestic Violence occurred since the civilized life came into existence on this planet (Earth), Violence against women is a manifestation of unequal physical-power equation between men and women. Domestic Violence occurs as a repercussion of temperamental and behavioural-problems, poverty, social backwardness, and centuries old baseless cultural traditions.

Behind closed doors of homes all across the world people are being tortured, beaten and killed. Much too often, the culmination of a long and intense history of abuse at home is the killing of the female partner. Sometimes, the children's lives are also taken. And sometimes, to complete the orgy of violence, the man ends up taking his own life.

Article title "**What is domestic violence?**" describes Domestic Violence; "Domestic violence is the willful intimidation, physical assault, battery, sexual assault, and/or other abusive behavior as part of a systematic pattern of power and control perpetrated by one intimate partner against another. It includes physical violence, sexual violence, psychological violence, and emotional abuse. The frequency and severity of domestic violence can vary dramatically; however, the one constant component of domestic violence is one partner's consistent efforts to maintain power and control over the other.

Domestic violence is an epidemic affecting individuals in every community, regardless of age, economic status, sexual orientation, gender, race, religion, or nationality. It is often accompanied by emotionally abusive and controlling behavior that is only a fraction of a systematic pattern of dominance and control. Domestic violence can result in physical injury, psychological trauma, and in severe cases, even death. The devastating physical, emotional, and psychological consequences of domestic violence can cross generations and last a lifetime."..........

Manifestation of persisting gender bias can be seen in s*ex ratio* of 917 girls to 1000 boys (According to 2011 census) and the crime-rate, as reported by National Crime Records Bureau, NCRB, from 8.8% in 2007 to 9.4 during 2011. (Leaving aside innumerable unreported-cases) Times of India (August 25, 2013, p.6) reports crime against women up by 7.1% since 2010.

UNICEF Reports on Progress of Nations released jointly by Government of India and UNICEF says that more than 60 million women, who should have been alive today, are missing. Responsible factors are from feticide to domestic violence to dowry deaths to physical assaults. Discrimination starts even before women are born and continue till they die. It exists in the form of –**Feticide** – Some new forms of violence have appeared with technological advances as is evident in case of female feticide, reflecting in adverse sex-ratio. Social bias in favor of a male-child lead to abortions (out of 8000 cases of abortions following sex-determination tests, 7999 are female fetus, according to a Survey) Sex-ratio is continuously declining allover India except for its southern province Kerala. Inefficient and ineffective performance of political, administrative and economic structures and mechanisms failed to stop it.

Domestic violence — also called intimate partner violence; which occurs between people in an intimate relationship. Domestic violence can take many forms, including emotional, sexual and physical abuse and threats of abuse. Men are sometimes abused by partners, but domestic violence is most often directed towards women. Domestic violence can happen in heterosexual or same-sex relationships. It might not be easy to identify domestic violence at first. While some relationships are clearly abusive from the outset, abuse often starts subtly and gets worse over time. You might be experiencing domestic violence if you're in a relationship with someone who: "Calls you names, insults you or puts you down," "Prevents or discourages you from seeing family members or friends," "Tries to control how you spend money, where you go, what medicines you take or what you wear."

If you're lesbian, bisexual or transgender, you might also be experiencing domestic violence if you're in a relationship with someone who: "Threatens to tell friends, family, colleagues or community members about your sexual orientation or gender identity."

Article title **"JHM Global Scotland' ending violence against women"** articulate rather well in its report, the reason and causes of brutal domestic violence in Pakistan, India and Africa: **"Domestic Violence in Pakistan**: Domestic abuse & domestic violence in Pakistan is very common. Killing, burning and maiming victims is not outside of the psyche of perpetrators in Pakistan. Extreme violence is part of society and not shocking to see it happen. Religious belief that empowers a husband's beating of his wife does not help the problem at all. Spousal abuse while being the most commonly reported form of domestic violence probably makes up for very little proportion of the collective statistics on domestic violence because domestic violence encompasses all sorts of abuses in a household. It includes child abuse, intimate partner violence (IPV) and domestic violence and other forms of abuse.

Domestic Violence in India: United Nation Population Fund Report stated that:
1] Two-third of married Indian women are victims of domestic violence.
2] As many as 70 per cent of married women in India between the age of 15 and 49 are victims of beating, rape or forced sex.
3] More than 55 percent of the women suffer from domestic violence, especially in the states of Bihar, Utter Pradesh and other northern states.
The violence used in India to treat women comes on a higher scale amongst nations whose culture & religion condones ill treatment of women. Brides are tormented due to dowry payment failure. Women who fail to give birth to sons instead of daughters are treated as useless, worthless and second class in a society where boys are more valued than girls. Many women have been tortured, set ablaze & burned alive, amputated or treated with extreme cruelty by whole families. It is appalling.

Domestic Violence in Africa: Domestic abuse & domestic violence is very common in Africa. Beating women, murder, and maiming victims is not unusual in many respect both in villages & in big cities across Africa. Violence is uncommon place and it is part of the society norm in many respect. War, political clashes & regular tribal & inter-tribal conflict have left a permission mentality for violence to be perpetrated and women are the weakest link and the commonest victims.

Most Common Causes: The most common causes for women stalking and battering include dissatisfaction with the dowry and exploiting women for more of it, arguing with the partner, refusing to have sex with him, neglecting children, going out of home without telling the partner, not cooking properly or on time, indulging in extra marital affairs, not looking after in-laws etc. In some cases infertility in females also leads to their assault by the family members. The greed for dowry, desire for a male child and alcoholism of the spouse are major factors of domestic violence against women in rural areas. There have been gruesome reports of young bride being burnt alive or subjected to continuous harassment for not bringing home the amount of demanded dowry. Women in India also admit to hitting or beating because of their suspicion about the husband's sexual involvement with other women."...........

Intimate partner violence is a considerable problem for any society, but its effects are particularly significant for migrant communities. In addition to the usual reasons men abuse women, it is fairly acknowledged that migration is a stressful process for migrants and it heightens the risk of women to experience domestic violence. In many cases, men in migrant communities mistreat their partners or spouses as a way to regain control and power in their lives, particularly when their migrant status has deprived them of this social standing.

Women in abusive relationships are often afraid to leave because they don't have anywhere to go, especially if they have children. Their financial and job situation may be precarious. Many female partners involved in domestic violence against women don't have credit on their own to be able to get an apartment, and since they've been abused for a long time, probably haven't been able to keep a steady job, and have a poor work history, making it even more difficult to survive on their own.

Statistics show that low-income women, minorities, and young women are most often the targets of domestic violence against women. Women under 24 are among the highest numbers for rape cases. One out of every five women in the United States will be raped or be the victim of an attempted rape while she's in college.

Statistics also reveal that the lower the income a household has, the more likely that domestic violence in the home will occur. African American and Native American women have the highest risk of being domestic abuse victims by the men they are in a relationship with.

Violence against women and children has continued unabated. And the culture that helps to makes violence against women permissible, even something to be celebrated, remains unaddressed.

Moreover, the cultural messages that eroticism violence against women and make it appear sexy, is the same culture in which survivors of sexual assault have to survive. What happened to them is made into something others call art and fashion.

Media, advertising and popular culture reflect values. Any reading of the social landscape tells us that women are really only good for one thing: to be used sexually. The proliferation and globalization of sexual imagery, often overlaid with violence, is a cause of distress for sexual assault survivors, those who care for them and those working to end violence against women. Colonising the public space with images that approve and perhaps even incite sexual violence, creates and shapes attitudes. Yet government and regulatory bodies for the most part allow it to go on. How can violence against women be addressed effectively if the advertising, marketing, music, clothing, and gaming industries continue to treat it as chic fashion and fun, like something that is just so hot right now?

There is another perspective and much bigger perspective with regards to sexual violence and domestic violence, Late Marriages or significantly large percentage of modern day Women preferring to maintain single marital status either for protracted period of time or permanently. Sexually deprived and sex starvation could also potentially have disastrous social consequence in society.

Imaging smelling good food you know that you cannot eat. This is probably a pleasant experience, if you've had enough other good food to eat lately. But it might be a painful experience if you were starving, or had long been living on a bland diet of rice and beans.

Similarly, being around attractive sexy people is often a pleasant experience, but probably feels quite different when it is clear to all that you have zero chance of attracting them, and if you feel severely deprived of satisfying sex. And while our society is rich enough that few starve for food anymore, wealth is much less able to prevent sexual starvation.

So our society has far more sex-starved than food-starved folks. Yet it is far more acceptable to publicly lament the plight of the food starved than the sex starved. Signalling compassion is not about helping the needy.

The supreme moment in a woman's life, when her original nature, her natural desire manifests itself, is that in which her own sexual union takes place. She embraces the man passionately and presses him to her; it is the greatest joy of passivity, stronger even than the contented feeling of a hypnotised person, the desire of matter which has just been formed, and wishes to keep that form for ever. That is why a woman is so grateful to her possessor, even if the gratitude is limited to the moment, as in the case of prostitutes with no memory, or, if it lasts longer, as in the case of more highly differentiated women.

Both men and women have their own unique challenges. The challenge of the man is not to let his energy run wild, and the challenge of the woman is not to let her energy run dry. Whereas men needs to reach perfection, women needs to maintain it.

For a lot of men, his woman is the only place he can go to for connection and love. His woman is often the only source he has. Men have many challenges in the world – and it's important that he has a woman who understands his needs. **Of course** – understanding a man's needs is not about just giving him sex. Men have many other needs, too. **But the issue of sex is one that many women struggle with.**

And, the modern western world has been affected by the feminist movement which has given women the idea *that they shouldn't prioritize a man's needs,* and that includes not wanting to meet his sexual needs regularly. However, the man is still expected to meet *her* needs!

Sex is one of the major and most important ways through which a man gets his needs of connection/love met. Men aren't just asking for sex because it feels good (although that's part of it too).

The emotional infancy of twenty something men — contrasted with the personal and professional focus of women their age — is the result of our collective cultural decision that it isn't taboo to have sex before marriage. In western society so many creative-class young men are "taking advantage of a social landscape in which sex has been decoupled from marriage but biology hasn't been abolished,"

But fertility is a legitimate back-of-the-mind anxiety for many young women, and we tend to imagine (explicitly or otherwise) timelines for ourselves as we try to navigate the limitations of biology.

Article title **"Can feminism Save Marriage?"** writes: "According to **new Pew data**, the percentage of Americans who have never married is at an all-time high: As of 2012, 1 of 5 adults 25 or over has never wed. In the 1960s, by contrast, the number was just 1 adult in 10. Liberal and conservative commentators alike point to feminism, and the increased gender equality that came with it, as a primary cause or culprit, depending on whether they're giving the movement credit or blame. But lower marriage rates don't mean that Americans today are a sea of depressed, unstable singles. Quite the opposite: There are more single people because we're marrying later than ever before and building alternative family structures. And for many of us, that's a great thing — **it means** more stable marriages, happier unions, and healthier families. For some others, though, declining marriage rates takes a heavy toll. And feminism may just be the answer.

The threat of spinsterhood has long been used as a warning against women gaining too much independence or power. In 1986, Newsweek **published an incendiary article** claiming that a 30-year-old college-educated woman had just a 20 percent chance of marrying; by 35, her prospects decreased to 5 percent; and that if a woman was still single on her 40th birthday, she had a better chance of being killed by a terrorist than walking down the aisle. That wasn't exactly true then, and today it couldn't be further from reality: College-educated women are not only the most likely group of women to get married, but they're the most likely to stay **married**. Part of the reason is that they're marrying at older ages, which means they're more financially stable, more mature, and have more experience navigating relationships. College-educated women also tend to marry college-educated men, which means their households typically have more money and they don't face the same stressors that can destabilize marriages between couples who are living in poverty or even just getting by. And college-educated women are much likelier to delay childbearing until after marriage, which also contributes to more stable relationships. According to **a new book** by researcher Isabel Sawhill, these highly educated couples are also more likely to have gender-egalitarian marriages and to plan their families, which leads to higher rates of marital happiness."............

Now to understand the consequences of Late/delayed Marriage from different perspective; It creates peculiar kinds and types of social problems when some women prefer career over family, now, when a woman delays her pregnancy or when she opts to get married any time after her age has passed 38 years, and when a woman plans to start her family after she's reached 40 years of age, in which case that women will experience many kinds of health problems, because once the woman is over the age of 38 years as it is she will be close to approaching menopausal, obviously conceiving child after the age of 40 won't be without a hitch, but more importantly let us understand it from social angle.

When, if, a woman who becomes pregnant for the first time at the age of 41years, Now, that woman delivers her first child when her age is about 42 years or thereabout, now this woman who becomes mother at the age of 42, so, when the woman will be 62 years old, her daughter's age will be 20 years, now this is what I mean to explain what causes peculiar types of social and internal family problems, when there are parents and children in our society who have huge age difference between them, if, for example; mothers age is 62 years and her daughter's age is 20 years, it's a big generation gap, hence, in such a scenario, for a 62 year old mother to discipline and inhibit her daughter, it will not be as easy a thing to do, therefore in such situations either the mother adopts a very aggressive approach towards her daughter, or considering that she's too old and in her sixties in such case mothers finds themselves extremely feeble and just gives their daughter freedom and allows her to take own decisions and make choices regarding her life.

So, in both cases and instances whether because of mother's aggressive approach or because of soft attitude could potentially prove devastatingly harmful for young daughter who is at critical juncture of her life at 20 years of age, with no appropriate assistance and guidance from her mother, in such cases it is highly likely that young daughters could potentially go astray.

When there is a huge age difference and big generation gap between children and their parents, it becomes difficult to strike chord and to balance personal and social responsibility between them, as both children and parents can't understand life from each other's perspective, difference of perception affects family stability, losing temper and patience becomes normal thing, children from dysfunctional families and children who are victim of domestic violence, such children under frustration becomes more vulnerable and susceptible to adopt unethical and unconventional methods of life.

Article title "**Shame Speaks Volumes About Domestic Violence Against Men,**" writes: "Domestic violence is a most serious, prevalent subject for all of us to be aware of. We often hear of the domestic violence against women, but we do not always hear about it from a man's perspective. In fact, more than 1 in 4 men (28.5%) in the United States have experienced rape, physical violence, and/or stalking by an intimate partner in their lifetime. The reason we do not always hear about this side of the issue is because many male domestic violence victims under-report the crimes against them due to shame and embarrassment. Shame is a short film that hopes to spread awareness and empower men to report their victimization. You can see a short trailer of the film, which was released on October 1st, the beginning of domestic violence awareness month, through Distrify.com. I can tell you the trailer, although short, packs a powerful message and intrigues you to see Shame in its entirety."................

Until now, there was talk about the phenomenon of violence most often in the context of a woman – the victim and the men – the perpetrator, while statistics show that the phenomenon of violence by women against men is just as common. The problem of domestic violence on the part of women is ignored, marginalized, considered to be less harmful. Often violence against her husband will be ignored, because it is in terms of the perception of the majority of society.

Domestic violence, also referred to as intimate partner violence, against men is happening far more than what is being reported to the police. Research studies have confirmed that society's traditional view of males as the stronger sex and females as the weaker counterpart do contribute to the cause of unreported violence against male victims. Because of society's perspective, male victims of domestic violence are being subjected to life-threatening violence, emotional distress and discrimination. In addition, studies have shown that supportive resources do not exist for male domestic violence victims as they do for female victims, this further contributes to the attacks going unreported.

Someone in the U.S. experiences sexual violence every 2 minutes, about 60 percent of these assaults are often left unreported, according to the Rape Abuse and Incest National Network. "We live in a society in which gendered violence is so normalized and sometimes even glorified," Women's Studies Assistant professor Anh Hua said. "Much healing is needed for the perpetrators as well as the survivors of gendered violence. We have failed to revere, honour, value and respect women, elders and even children at the local, national and global levels. The majority of sexually violent cases occur between people with a pre-existing relationship, and most of these cases involve the consumption of alcohol. "If people especially the young men and women choose to consume alcohol, they should make sure that they are not consuming so much that their awareness, judgment, or ability to give proper consent is hindered." The misconception that sexual violence occurs in a dark alley with a stranger instead of with someone you know, care about and trust makes the situation harder to accept and even more difficult to report.

Sadly, most men falsely believe they are more sexual than women, proving that they know neither women nor themselves. Consequences? They're forever doomed to grovel for sex and succumb in every battle. Typical of how most men think: *Women attract men more easily than men attract women because men's urges are stronger.* He couldn't be more wrong. It amazes me how many men actually believe that their sexual urges exceed those of women. **Totally untrue.** So, all of their behaviours, in the quest to get female affection and approval, are based on this myth. Ironically, instead of getting affection and approval from women, they lose power and money to them.

When a man kowtows to a woman, just to get laid, she will rule every aspect of his life — forever. Yet, the typical man will yield to her. Why? Two reasons:

1- Ignorance about female sexuality
2- Knowledge of female sexuality but lacking the courage to act on it — fear of rejection.

Our **Brain** is important for sexuality because of the chemistry, but it's also important for ideas. It helps how you experience pleasure and how you define it.

Similarly like domestic violence, teen dating violence is a pattern of controlling, and abusive behaviours of one person over another within a **romantic relationship**. It can include verbal, emotional, physical, sexual, and **financial abuse**. It can occur in both heterosexual and homosexual relationships. It knows no boundaries and crosses race, **socio-economic status**, culture, and religion. Violence can happen to anyone. Like adults, teenagers can choose better relationships when they learn to identify the early warning signs of an **abusive relationship**, understand that they have choices, and believe they are valuable people who deserve to be treated with dignity and respect.

A great deal of ink has been spilled in recent times over a new "date rape detection nail polish" called Undercover Colors.

While its creators' hearts may have been in the right place, it is difficult to get excited over yet another thing that can and will be used to shift responsibility — and therefore blame — onto victims of sexual assault.

Women are already told to dress a certain way, travel in groups, watch their drinks, stay out of certain parts of town and never to accept drinks from strangers.

Women and girls are advised to wear shoes they can run in, carry keys in their fists, and always, always make sure to tell someone where we're going.

Asking victims why they didn't try harder to avoid becoming victims implies an even more insidious follow-up question: Didn't you want not to be raped?

Not only does this place, the onus for avoiding assault squarely on the victim, but it subtly encourages doubting whether or not victims were victims at all.

This, in turn, serves to embolden those who falsely claim that there is an epidemic of women who "cry rape" because they regretted consensual sex the next morning.

The rigorous questioning faced by those who come forward discourages others from reporting the crime when it happens to them. The ripple effects are tremendous.

Furthermore, Undercover Colors reinforces the myth that stranger rape is the most common — which is categorically false — and ignores the fact that the No. 1 one date-rape drug of choice is plain old alcohol.

Date-rape drugs are symptomatic of enormous cultural flaws regarding the way we treat women, consent and sex. These products do nothing to fix that. Their glowing reception is grossly disproportionate to their usefulness.

"While date rape drugs are often used to facilitate sexual assault, very little science exists for their detection," the team, known as Undercover Colors, wrote on their **Facebook page**. "Our goal is to invent technologies that empower women to protect themselves from this heinous and quietly pervasive crime."

Young adults dance the night away at all-night parties commonly referred to as raves. Although raves may seem like innocent fun, some party-goers bring dangerous substances to these parties. Together, these substances are called club drugs; individually they are sometimes referred to as "G," "Roofies," "Special K," "Acid," or "Ecstasy." One of the most common abuse patterns is the use **of Rohypnol as a rape drug**. Rohypnol is known as a rape drug because perpetrators reportedly slip it into victim's drinks causing them to blackout. Rohypnol takes away a victim's normal inhibitions, leaving the victim helpless and blocking the memory of a rape or assault. Only 10 minutes after ingesting Rohypnol, a person may feel dizzy, disoriented, too hot or cold and nauseated. They may also have a difficult time speaking and eventually, the victim will pass out. The person will then have no recollection of the events that occurred.

When people think of rape, they might picture a stranger jumping out of a shadowy place and attacking someone. But in reality about half of all people who are raped know the person who attacked them. This is known as date rape. Girls and women are more likely to be raped, but it can also happen to guys. It's not just men who rape. In rare cases, women rape, too. Being good friends, talking to someone, dating, or hooking up usually *don't* lead to violence or rape. But it can happen, so it's best to be prepared.

Date rape is also extremely common -- according to one study, nearly 1/3 of rapes are committed by a date. When you're dating someone new, understand that No absolutely means No, and don't ever let anyone make you feel guilty about knowing what you do and don't want. Don't be afraid to communicate your needs clearly and loudly, if necessary. The majority of rapes in college occur during the first few weeks of your freshman and sophomore years. These are the riskiest days because people are just getting to know each other, there are a lot of new people around, along with an abundance of alcohol. Though this shouldn't keep you from having fun or leaving your dorm room, you should be extra cautious about meeting new people, and make sure that you stick with your friends and your sound judgment.

Because women generally have less body mass and water content than men, they become intoxicated faster. They also become addicted sooner. The higher Blood

Alcohol Level (BAL) in women not only impairs them more when they drink, but it also accelerates damage to the brain and other organs. The mortality rate for **chemically dependent women** is 50-100 times higher than their male counterparts. Oftentimes drug and alcohol addiction in women is tied into their relationships. Women have an instinctive need for connection; they are biologically wired to sustain, nurture and respond to relationships. When primary relationships are ruptured by physical abuse, sexual abuse or abandonment, women tend to experience the distress, pain or suffering associated with such ruptures as a **trauma**. As a result, they often self-medicate to alleviate symptoms of **post-traumatic stress disorder** (PTSD). Trauma breeds more trauma.

For many women, rape is a crime where the after-effects of PTSD is felt even years later, it can be as bad as the assault itself. Experts agree that suicide can result from rape related PTSD, just as it can cause suicide thoughts and actions immediately after sexual assault.

If you have experienced sexual assault by an intimate partner, it can be challenging to come forward for many reasons. You may be concerned for your safety or the safety of your children, still have strong feelings for your partner, or aren't convinced that what's happening to you is really sexual assault. It's understandable to feel this way. Sexual assault in a relationship rarely exists in a vacuum. It often occurs alongside other forms of abusive behaviour. Ending an abusive relationship is not something that you have to do alone. Reaching out for help from friends, loved ones, local organizations or law enforcement can help you through this process.

Sorry, but the cat is out of the bag here—this is a really, really massive cultural problem.

The fact that 20 percent of women on a college campus will be a victim of **sexual assault** is hard to prove, not because it is based on fiction, but because despite the fact that more people are speaking out, victims are still scared to come forward. Sadly, the number is probably higher. People fear they will be blamed. They fear they will not be believed. They fear they will lose friends. At times, because our culture is so flawed, that in most cases victims fears and thinks it's perhaps their fault.

Workplace domestic violence; Domestic violence doesn't stay at home – it can strike at work as well. Domestic violence has a profound impact on business. Workplace safety is compromised when an employee is in an abusive relationship, as it's not uncommon for abusers to seek out their partner at work, endangering her, co-workers and customers on the scene.

Likewise, victims enduring domestic violence are often distracted at work, making errors, missing deadlines and generally underperforming. Physical injuries interfere with labour requirements, while forcing higher healthcare expenses. Indeed, victims of domestic violence are said to miss as many as 8 million paid work days annually.

The National Network to End Domestic Violence (NNEDV) advises that domestic violence is estimated to cost employers in the United States up to $13 billion a year.

Given its impact on workplace safety and the bottom line, employers need to recognize the disturbing realities of domestic violence. Another reality: 70 percent of businesses have no formal policy addressing domestic violence.

Career seekers and employees should be aware of the fact that an employer's business culture may actually create an environment that breeds job violence and puts everyone at risk. When companies have an attitude of harassment and intimidation instead of co-operation towards their workplace, negative consequences usually follows.

Some forms of workplace violence enter from outside the immediate working environment, such as a criminal or domestic violence situations and it is important to understand that domestic violence does not discriminate. It occurs within all age ranges, ethnic backgrounds, economic levels and genders, though domestic violence is predominantly against women. Although the violence may not occur within your property, the impacts are real. Whether it is harassing phone calls, taking time off due to injuries sustained from a partner, or a decrease in productivity because of this extremely stressful situation, it is critical that domestic abuse be seen as a serious issue. Raising awareness in the workplace is essential.

There are many workplace-specific signs and symptoms that are often a pattern rather than a single indication. These include arriving early or late to work, decreased productivity, tension around receiving repeated personal phone calls, concentration problems, bruises and other bodily pain complaints and even flowers or gifts sent to the employee for no apparent reason.

Domestic abuse is the abuse of power and control over one person by another and can take many different forms, including physical, sexual, emotional, verbal and financial abuse. I find it alarming given the prevalence of domestic violence (1 in 4 women will experience domestic violence) that few employers are addressing it as a workplace issue. One in four women will experience domestic abuse at some point in their lifetime. This means it is likely that all workplaces will have staff that have experienced or are experiencing domestic abuse as well as those who are perpetrators of abuse. After all, homicide is the second leading cause of death for women in the workplace. Employers have a duty to protect their employees from harm in the workplace. From a bottom line, preventing domestic violence and promoting safety is good for business. Flexible work arrangements can be a vital part of workplace safety planning. This may be as simple as asking your employer to adjust rosters to vary your days or start and finish times. It may involve time off to get a protection order that will protect you, the kids, your home and your workplace. Or it may involve moving for a while to a branch or area of the workplace that's not exposed to the public. Flexible work arrangements involve a safe and honest discussion about what mangers and employers can offer their staff to support them through the crisis. Flexible work arrangements mean employers reassure their staff: "we understand, your job is safe, and let's discuss what you need."

We are haunted by our mistakes and crippled by guilt and regret. Shame fractures our relationships, sabotages our confidence in judiciary and hinders our ability to move forward in life. Our war against shame will not be won in a single battle. It will be an ongoing process, but through the renewal of our minds and shifting our patterns, Nature has given us the power to be transformed.

While financial factors contribute to the problem, the causes of domestic violence involve psychological issues that we must deal with in order to stop the cycle of abuse. There are emotional dynamics that contribute greatly to domestic violence. It involves a destructive thought process (or "critical inner voice") that abusers experience both towards themselves and their partners, thoughts like "You're not a man if you don't control her" or "She is making a fool out of you."

Being challenged by a relationship partner can be distressing, arousing fear and anger for some people. In these instances, whether they are experiencing an insult, a perceived threat, or an extreme provocation, both men and women who engage in domestic violence are very often acting on their "**critical inner voice**." This "voice" is a destructive thought process in which people are telling themselves negative things about themselves and of their partners. The more a person listens to these thoughts, the more they feed feelings of being wronged and of needing to retaliate, sometimes escalating to a point of becoming violent. In addition to listening to this critical inner voice, couples involved in domestic violence have often forged a destructive connection, an illusion that they cannot live without each other. There is a feeling of merged identity between the couple, in which both partners do not feel they can stand on their own without the other. This illusion contributes to what we call a "**fantasy bond**." This unhealthy feeling of fusion makes it difficult for a couple to break free from the relationship, even after it has become hostile or dangerous. It also makes it easier for a couple to abuse each other, as they begin to see each other as extensions of themselves and not as separate individuals, who they are hurting.

The formation of a fantasy bond further encourages the attitude that one person can define or victimize another person in some way. It also supports the idea that one partner in a couple has power or control over the other. Thus, people are more likely to feel entitled, mistreated, and righteous in their anger towards their partner.

The social capital created by traditional families is what undergirds the rest of our society. Sociologists and economists now understand that when this social capital is diminished, it causes all sorts of other problems. The crises of the welfare state, wage stagnation, income inequality, unemployment, the prison-industrial complex — all of these, and much more, can be traced to the breakdown of the family. The "**fragmented family**" refers to more than just the 50% of marriages that end in divorce, but also to the fact that many children never really have a family, since they are raised by mothers who have never married. It is not easy to come up with a precise number, but it is certainly true that, of the children who escape being aborted in the United States, the majority will not be raised by their married biological parents; one parent is likely to be missing, and it is usually the father.

The so-called "permissive or swinging sixties" has become a metaphor for contemporary social conflict. For progressive it has heralded as a time of revolutionary ferment which ushered in much needed social change, ushering in the civil rights movements, decolonisation, women's liberation, gay and lesbian liberation, green and peace movements. For conservative it has become a scapegoat to blame many contemporary problems upon issues such as pornography, marriage breakdowns, single parent families, welfare state dependency, drugs and youth crimes are all seen as having their origins in the "permissiveness" of the sixties (1960s). For the generations after sixties, the love children of the baby boomers, it is often seen as a failed project which sustains their parents Romanticisation of their youth prior to "selling out."

The Sexual Revolution of the 1960s, in whose aftermath we all live, billed itself as an attempt to sweep away the fire-and-brimstone Puritanism it attributed to the previous era. Yet it turned itself into a twisted mirror image of that very Puritanism. This sort of thing happens all the time, on both the left and the right: the other side draws a caricature of you, and you "defy" them by embracing the caricature. The advocates of the Sexual Revolution agree that sex is dirty, filthy, disgusting, meaningless, impersonal, and brutishly physical—but **they're for it**!

The Sexual Revolution was not just about removing artificial impediments to sexual enjoyment. What it advocated was not merely sex without guilt, but sex that is "**zipless**," i.e., "without emotional involvement or commitment." It is sex without meaning, context, consequences—or human connection.

This is quite perverse, when you think about it. You have a movement that says it is in favour of sex, which then tries to empty sexuality of all value and significance. They seek to liberate sex by trivializing it.

One of the consequences is the well-documented **death spiral of the pornography addict** who needs more and more stimulation—something weirder, more shocking, more over-the-top—just to get the same level of arousal, like a drug addict who acquires resistance and needs higher and higher doses. When sex is trivialized and deprived of meaning, people have to find some way to fill the emptiness. Some of them will try to make it up on volume.

But after the 1960s, liberation wasn't just about enjoying sex. It was about sticking it to The Man. All of this leads us to the dead end of the Sexual Revolution, in which sex has become all about the least sexy thing on earth. It's no longer about defying joyless authority figures, because there is no authority figure more joyless than the campus feminist. Instead, it's about "smashing the patriarchy."

"No man is above the law and no man is below it; nor do we ask any man's permission when we ask him to obey it." Theodore Roosevelt first spoke these words more than a century ago, but they're as true today as they ever were. In our criminal justice system, everyone one should be treated fairly—men and women, cops and criminals, and people of all nationalities and backgrounds.

One problem creates another problem, the problems with problem is that it just keeps adding On, worldwide there are many recurring social problems, for which society is simply failing to find any amicable solution to contain the harmful effects of it, physical violence occurs in many different form, most notable among them are "Honour killing, force marriage, force prostitutions, FGM (female genital mutilation/cutting), but most severe of all is **Vitriolic acid attack**," acid a flammable material thrown on women with nefarious intention to destroy her beautiful looks and to disfigure her irresistible body.

The Arab women often suffer domestic violence, including so-called "honour killing," behind a societal cloak of silence. Stricter Islamic law implemented in most Arab countries restrict women's personal liberties, for example by giving them lesser status than husbands in divorce proceedings and requiring the permission of a husband or father to work, travel or borrow from a bank.

Often, women's issues are trivialised into whether or not to wear the veil or shake hands with men outside their family, and while larger issues, such as domestic violence, are being the central issue of what "equality" means and how it is expressed go largely ignored. For example, domestic violence is wrong because it creates pain and suffering and is unjust, but the central belief of a man's right to rule over his wife is not always part of this discussion.

The predicament of Arab women is the region longstanding patriarchal tradition of protection and "honour" wrapped into tribal identity. The Authoritarian regimes that emerged with Arab independence a half century ago have undermine the liberal institution and values that might have better encouraged women's rights and protected under a rule of law.

In some Muslim circles, the "F" word (feminism) raises as many tensions as eyebrows, immediately conjuring images of the dominating, angry, family-hating woman. But like other images that comes to mind upon mention of any label, including the image of the oppressed woman that often comes to mind when one hears "Muslim," this gut reaction is based on stereotypes that may be true in a very specific historical and social context, but does not hold water when compared to a larger reality, and therefore does not justify the hostility that follows. Important distinction. "Islamic feminism" is not simply a feminism that is born from Muslim cultures, but one that engages Islamic theology through the text and canonical traditions.

In Iraq a 17 year old girl Du'a Khalil Aswad was brutally stoned to death, "an abhorrent murder," her fault was that she felt in love with a teenage boy who was from different religion, to her dismay, Miss Aswad while she was being stoned to death the local city Iraqi security force witnessed the incident of Du'a being stoned to death yet did nothing to stop it, Miss Aswad, a member of minority Kurdish group called Yezidi, was condemned to death as "Honour killing" by other men in her family and other Hardline religious leaders because of her intimate relationship with a boy who was from Sunni Muslim community, Du'a Khalil Aswad was drag outside her house by 8 or 9 men and was stoned for nearly half an hour till she died.

Such incident of stoning young girls and women are becoming more common, extreme barbaric sharia laws are practiced in the jihadist (holy warrior) terrorist group ISIS controlled areas in Iraq and Syria, many incident of stoning girls to death are videotaped and released on social media site like Youtube.

The use of **capital punishment in Saudi Arabia** is based on Sharia (or Islamic law) and is prominent internationally because of the wide range of crimes which can result in the death penalty and because it is usually carried out by public beheading. In 2011, the Saudi government reported 26 executions in the country. Unlike executions in most other countries that have not abolished the death penalty, executions of offenders are not performed privately in prisons, but publicly in central Riyadh, and have been called the "only form of public entertainment" in Saudi Arabia "apart from football matches."

Saudi Arabia has a criminal justice system based on a hard-line and literal form of Sharia law reflecting a particular state-sanctioned interpretation of Islam.

In one of such incident: Rizana Nafeek a young nanny from Sri Lanka, was beheaded by sword in January 2013 in Saudi Arabia, punishment for allegedly killing a baby in 2007 when she was believed to be just 17. The execution spurred international outcry, given Nafeek's age at the time of the incident and her limited access to a defence attorney. The beheading has also shined a light on the Arab kingdom's medieval system of punishment, which includes cutting the hands off thieves, executing women accused of adultery, and flogging men accused of being gay.

Few details of Nafeek's execution have leaked from the country's tightly controlled media, but the interior ministry said her head was severed from her body in public in Dawadmy, a dusty suburb of the capital Riyadh.

In modern times, women in Saudi Arabia condemned to death were traditionally executed by gunfire, but in recent years they have routinely been beheaded, an historic form of execution ordered under sharia, or the Muslim religious law that governs the country. The death penalty is routinely allowed for criminals convicted of murder, rape, armed robbery, drug trafficking or drug use, and apostasy or the renunciation of the Islamic faith, according to human rights group Amnesty International.

Some 82 executions were carried out in Saudi Arabia in the year 2012, according to Amnesty. It is unknown how many of them were women or carried out by sword, but the majority of the condemned were foreigners, like Nafeek. Beheadings in Saudi Arabia are governed by certain rules. They are conducted in public, typically in town squares or near prisons. The condemned, as well as the executioner, typically wear white. The convict is blindfolded, handcuffed and often given a sedative. A plastic tarp, several feet wide, is sometimes spread out around the convict to make cleaning up the blood and recovering her head easier.

Over the past 100 years or more, many feminist movement have strived hard to win battle of wits against their opposite sex gender. Women have indeed made significant progress, girls and women are doing remarkably well professionally, they have high income jobs, women are skilled professionals and owns businesses, whether in fashion world or corporate world, even in agriculture or Aerospace women have found space for themselves and many a females have become principle breadwinners for their family, despite all that women have proved they are No less courageous and are equally competitive in almost every field and arena as good as men or maybe given a chance to prove they could prove to be more productive than men. But, yet, with heavy heart I have to say, that even in this day and age around the world most people are living with generations old primitive mind set, particularly in highly densely populated countries like India and Pakistan you will find extremely backward thinking outrageously superstitious and savagely conservative people.

In countries such as India and Pakistan most people belonging to either affluent class or underclass social background, talk about economically backward or wealthy families, they are both equal offenders and on same page when it comes to thinking with regards to girl child, most of the people particularly in India and Pakistan subtly, covertly or overtly considers birth of a girl child in their families as jinx and inauspicious, their insular beliefs considers it is a curse to have girl child born into their family, many parents considers girl child to be burden on them as they believe daughters are liability for their parents, because girls are no good and can't become breadwinners for their family, therefore you will read and listen lots of real life stories of brazen and brutal parents of beleaguered infant girl child in countries like India, Pakistan or even Afghanistan ruthlessly getting Rid of their infant daughter by either killing infant girl child or throw her in Trash-bin or leaves her on railway platform as soon as she's born, the killings are executed in most dreadful manner, shameless and callous parents don't hesitate one bit in killing their daughter by stoning her to death using grinding stone or smash her to wall, gosh, it is really horrendous but to our dismay, it is true, that, parents kills or get rid of their daughters in bizarrely inhuman and barbaric of way, it is a heart rending fact.

There is nothing in any religious book which sanctions honour killing but even then Hundreds, if not thousands, of women are murdered by their families each year in the name of family "honour." It's difficult to get precise numbers on the phenomenon of honour killing, the murders frequently go unreported, the perpetrators unpunished, and the concept of family honour justifies the act in the eyes of some societies. Honour Killing concept came to light in India just because the media highlighted the issue with responsibility. But the concept is not new its existence is as old as society. The reason behind the honour killing is still same i.e. women are considered as a vessel of the family reputation.

"Honour" works to restrict women's autonomy, particularly sexual autonomy within male-dominated societies which place a high value on women's chastity. Within "honour" crimes, families may collaborate to commit violence against a relative who is thought to have violated the restrictions around female behaviour. Such violations might include dress or make-up which is not approved by the family, resisting an arranged marriage, seeking divorce, reporting domestic violence and some so-called offences may appear trivial.

Honour killings most often involve young women attempting to break from the pre-modern cultural traditions of their immigrant families — families plunged into the maelstrom of increasingly post-modern secular society. (The occasional male victims tend to be accused of adultery and homosexuality as well as rape, exhibitionism and paedophilia.) In most cases, perpetrators of honour killings appear motivated by deeply held moral convictions and seek to restrict the influence of Western values, especially involving dress, socialisation and sexuality.

Jilted lover, one sided love affair, voracious husband who is unhappy because his wife has not his met dowry demand or if husband suspect his wife of Adultery, or drug addict/alcoholic or religious fundamentalist insular brother and father: well, these issues and reasons becomes catalyst for men to commit one of the most inhuman and wickedest of crime a human can think of or commit, that is; **Acid Attack on a Woman with intention to Disfigure her beautiful Looks**: Acid attack a vitriol attack or Vitriolage is a form of violent attack. This crime oft committed by a disgruntled person/persons (mostly are found to be man who either with help of his associates or his family members) to teach woman a lesson of her life to ruin her life once and for all, this crime otherwise committed all over the world but it is particularly common in countries like Pakistan, Afghanistan, Bangladesh and India, defined as the act of throwing acid or a similarly corrosive substance onto the body of another "with the intention to disfigure, maim, torture, or kill. It's a shocking crime, no matter where it's committed. Acid thrown in someone's face, leaving the victim burned, maimed and disfigured. Sadly, it happens more often than you think around the globe, and almost always, the victims are women. Perpetrators of these attacks throw acid at their victims, usually at their faces, burning them, and damaging skin tissues, often exposing and sometimes dissolving the bones. The long term consequences of these attacks may include blindness, as well as permanent scarring of the face and body, along with far-reaching social, psychological, and economic difficulties. The most common types of acid used in these attacks are sulphuric and nitric acid. Hydrochloric acid is sometimes used, but is much less damaging.

The reasoning behind heinous attacks is even more disturbing. Frequently, they occur because a woman wants a divorce from an abusive husband and he seeks to bring shame upon her for taking action against him. Steps are being taken to improve laws and prosecution for these crimes yet acid attack continues to be on rise. To elaborate further; Most acid-attacks are punishing measures towards women who have refused to accede to commands from men or have stood against abuses from them. The effects of these acid attacks upon their lives have been destructive: apart from the physical trauma undergone (some are scarred and maimed for life, despite numerous surgical interventions), they also have to face psychological trauma as well as social isolation and ostracism from their community. A law against acid crimes will hardly act as a deterrent when perpetrators know that if they have enough resources and leverage than they can shrug off any charge held against them, no matter the atrocity.

From the victims' point of view, there is a high risk of denial of justice, and the numerous obstacles they can face in their pursuit of justice may act as a strong disincentive preventing them from reporting the attacks. Indeed, the status of women in Pakistan, subject on the one hand to pressures not to disgrace their families by filing a case, and on the other hand, to disdain from the police officers themselves, will add to the obstacles faced by any average Pakistani seeking justice within a corrupted policing system and administration. Acid attacks are reported in many parts of the world. Since 1990s, Bangladesh has been reporting the highest number of attacks and highest incidence rates for women.

In addition to medical and psychological effects, many social implications exist for acid attack survivors, especially women. For example, such attacks usually leave victims handicapped in some way, rendering them dependent on either their spouse or family for everyday activities, such as eating and running errands. These dependencies are increased by the fact that many acid survivors are not able to find suitable work, due to impaired vision and physical handicap. This negatively impacts their economic viability, causing hardships on the families/spouses that care for them. As a result, divorce rates are high, with abandonment by husbands found in 25% acid assault cases in Uganda (compared to only 3% of wives abandoning their disfigured husbands. In some countries such as Saudi Arabia, Bahrain and Kuwait, acid attack victims are psychologically persecuted after the acid attack. The media overwhelmingly avoids reporting acid attack related violence; if covered, the description of the attack is minimized, blames the victims, omits women's voices, and treats sympathetically men who commit these crimes.

It has been reported on **Media News channel "CNN":** "It's the latest cruel tactic in the Pakistani Taliban's battle to stop girls and women from getting an education: acid thrown in their faces to scare them for life and deter others from following in their footsteps. The Pakistani Taliban have taken responsibility for the attacks and threatening pamphlets distributed around the city of Parachinar. They also warn local girls against going to school, "We will never allow the girls of this area to go and get a Western education," said Qari Muhavia, the local Pakistani Taliban leader, when contacted by CNN (media News Channel) by telephone. "If and when we find any girl from Parachinar going to university for an education we will target her (in) the same way, so that she might not be able to unveil her face before others," Muhavia said.

Shahab Uddin, a local government official from Kurram Agency in Pakistan's northern tribal belt, said the acid attack was the latest method used to terrorize young girls and deter them from going to school. Two girls, Zahida and Nabila, and one more boy had suffered burns, Uddin said, while Mohammad Ali, a fourth boy, was the student who was shot. "After throwing acid on the students the assailants opened fire on the van," Uddin said."----- CNN -------

The sundry array of "Islamic feminisms" throughout the Muslim world. Women in all these contexts are encountering the tradition based on their respective cultures, needs, priorities, and resources, creating a well-rounded picture of a global movement in which women create their own path to knowledge and move forward with it. In some contexts, this means addressing fundamental rights such as freedom from violence, while in others women carve out their own space and find room to challenge traditional dogma, rediscovering Islam's feminine history and room for future discourse.

There is a large disconnect between religious feminists and secular (non-religious) feminists, and that disconnect causes a lot of problems. Many religiously-minded feminists become offended at what they see as frankly ignorant critiques of their religion by secular feminists. Most recently, many debates have raged around

Muslim women who constantly feel that they have to defend their ideals and religious beliefs to western feminists, especially with certain issues like choosing to wear a hijab.

When people face a traumatic event or experience in life they often seek solace in something they believe in, something that will offer potential solutions and fill the emotional and spiritual vacuum when everything else has failed.

The vastly daunting task to expand women's participation in society will be to dismantle centuries-old discrimination. The Islamic establishment to remove cultural obstacles sanctified by religious rulings.

Domestic and sexual violence in Britain is little short of a national scandal, and it is time that British politicians said so. Women reported over 12million incidents of domestic abuse in year-2013. 3000 children a day in UK are witnessing violence in their own home. Two women a week are killed by their partner or an ex. It is a crime that we know affects men too, though on a much smaller scale.

In addition, thousands of girls are at risk of FGM, whilst others just disappear becoming victims of forced marriage or honour violence that we have been more comfortable turning a blind eye to. These crimes are a drain on country's economy and a blight on our society. Domestic abuse alone costs the UK £15.7 billion a year.

Feminism has argued that women are as intrinsically worthwhile as men on the basis that there are no differences between men and women. Yet this is patently untrue. As it turns out, while the differences don't mean that women or men are better than one another, it is in these differences that the reasons for men's oppression of women can be found. Moreover, because women could not understand men's anger and selfishness, they tended to be actively intolerant of it.

It's difficult to overestimate the impact that exploitation films have had on American and international cinema. This film genre is actually made up of many more specific subgenres that are commonly bound by characteristic over-the-top action, violence and sex. The fears and desires of both the viewer and the public are overtly exploited by the alternately (if not simultaneously) titillating and offensive scenes.

Without the vast galaxy of often X-rated exploitation films, also commonly referred to as **grindhouse pictures**, we wouldn't have many wider-released films and genres. Horror films like "Friday the 13th," respected revenge films like "The Accused" and classic teen romps like "Weird Science" may never have had precedence for runs in mainstream theatres had exploitation filmmakers not hacked even deeper into the jungle of taste and public perception.

Sexual Exploitation of Women in the Media Women are sexually exploited in the media. In today's society if people watch television programs such as Chingy featuring Snoop & Ludacris – Holidae; Charlie's Angels; the Z100 commercial with Britney Spears; or Baywatch they will see that the feminine image is presented differently than the masculine. In these programmes men are typically placed in sexual situations fully clothed, while women are presented in provocative clothing or less. The camera will frequently zoom in on body parts to focus on the woman's buttocks, midriff, and legs.

It seems that no matter where you look, women are being made into sexual objects. In movies, TV shows, music videos, video games and even news segments, women have to play up their sex appeal. This can be seen by the clothes women wear or the fact that they aren't given much character. Even when women *look* like they are being empowered in the media (like Angelina Jolie's 'Tomb Raider' character), they are often getting placed into a limited, hyper-sexualized role. There are very few representations of women in the media that a 'real woman' can actually relate to." Women often must be sexualized to be considered even a bit successful.

No matter your personal preference of what you find "pretty," we can all agree on a standard for beauty. If someone doesn't fit this ideal, they are less than, reduced to a second-class citizen. This affects men and women. If you don't fit the mould of what is attractive, then you are not worth anything. Being pretty gets you attention and fame, However this is, seemingly, the only way to gain fame and success. To become a sexual object for the media is the only way to have a voice in the media.

In the Article "**WPSP Institute for Women's Leadership in Latin America**," "Univision News Anchor Reporter **Leticia Gomez** believes that women have internalized the belief that their opinions need to be authorized by external sources. As a result of the institutional power structure in the media, women have been positioned to be compliments to men. Women are less likely to speak in assertive statements and will preface their opinions with "I think" or "I believe." Gomez suggests that women need to stop thinking that they need to be validated by men.

Many "women's issues" are characterizes as private troubles, issues that affect only a few individuals, rather than public issues, that affect the larger society. Gomez believes that economic and political institutions need to be addressed in order to expose private troubles. By bringing issues that affect women into the public sphere there is more opportunity to effect change and empower women."......

Excerpts from Article "**Exploitation of Women Research Papers**" writes; "It would be unbelievable if one day it was discovered that 50 percent of the world's population has remained basically repressed into invisibility for centuries. However, for centuries, academic and social resources, past and present, are filled with unfavourable images of this group and they are often still treated like objects and possessions. They have adorned public places since early Roman and Greek sculpture's displayed them on pedestals as the finest of artistic expression. Today many of those nude "artistic" images have become pornographic and are displayed publicly on street corners, in strip clubs, on television, in the movies and globally over the Internet. That 50 percent of the population so often disregarded is the feminine half of the human race.

In the fourth century B.C. Aristotle argued that women were deformities of nature. In the **Middle-Ages** and **Renaissance** period, women were defined as evil, sorcerers or witches if they expressed any intellectual or educational aspirations at all. Through business contracts, girls were passed from father to husband by apprenticeship or marriage as early as the age of twelve and the church laws not only permitted wife beating, but was known to support it more than a few times.

Male domination changed little through the centuries. Women were to be submissive and selfless in caring for the husbands and children's every wish.

A **17th century** female writer, Margaret Cavendish, described women's lives this way, "(men) would fain bury us in their houses or beds, as in a grave. The truth is, we live like bats or owls, labour like beasts, and die like worms". A century later another woman author, **Mary Wollstonecraft**, shared her social era's definition of women stating, "She was created to be the toy of man, his rattle, and it must jingle in his ears whenever, dismissing reason, he chooses to be amused".

We live three centuries later and men are still using women for their toys, paying for their services, abusing them whenever they choose to do so.".................

Today the women's liberation movement is under attack as increasingly the media proclaims the end of feminism. Efforts to drive back women's rights, gained over the past twenty five years, gather momentum. Attacks on women's control over their fertility and their bodies, unequal wages, domestic violence and sexual abuse, lack of access to decent jobs and continued discriminatory practices are all part of what has been termed the ``backlash'' against the women's movement.

Feminists themselves are divided about which way to proceed-whether to go on the offensive, or simply defend the gains of the past-or even to sacrifice the needs of the great majority of women in order to preserve gains for a privileged few.

Prostitution is not the world's oldest profession, as is commonly said, although it is probably one of the world's oldest forms of men's violence against women and girls. It seems old because men's sexual exploitation of women and children is ancient and defended as a part of men's natures that they have to have sex, even if it is purchased, forced or with a child. Prostitution is not natural or inevitable; it is abuse and exploitation of women and girls that results from structural inequality between women and men on a world scale. Prostitution Commodifies women and girls and markets their bodies for whatever acts men have sexualized and want to buy. Rarely are adult men treated this way.

Mother-hood is all about supreme sacrifice and benevolent, woman in a role of mother is supposed to give her child the best care and loving experience, of course mothers do give a lot love and affection to her children, there are many exemplary examples you will find, wherein woman as a mother has/had rendered utmost care and unflinching support to her children, but, with heavy heart I also have to mention that "Not" all mothers are the same, there are some nerve-wrecking examples of how evil and life threatening a woman as mother can be or has proven to be.

There are real life sordid stories of women in this world (living or death) who in the role of mother have proved to be example of extreme selfish and brutality. Covertly, overtly or subtly, Many mothers look in their children a potential benefit for themselves, particularly if they have a daughter, for many mothers they consider their daughters to be a money minting machine, yes, there are many mothers who sell their daughters or force their daughters into marriages for monetary gains, many mothers simply by persuasion or by exerting pressure forces their daughters into prostitution.

There are also many incidents and examples you'll discover if reported criminal cases are studied wherein the mothers have been found accused of plotting of eliminating her daughter, such murders/killings are often called Honour killings, well, if the books of registered criminal cases and media reports are opened you'll find millions of incidents that has happened over past hundreds of years which accentuates the gruesome nature of humans misdemeanour, we people at times are not safe among our own people, sometimes the victim of domestic violence don't realize it at all, but, even if they do notice and feels it, realize it, and are aware of the fact, as in, how we are being ill-treated or unfairly being dishonoured by our voracious family members and relatives, yet person who is suffering excruciating humiliation at home do not protest or open his/her mouth in public, instead, he/she tend to restrain him/herself and prefers to tolerate extreme pain.

When others harms us, we lament a lot, but, when people are cheated by their own near and dear ones, when our own people and our own family members systematically exploits us, it shatters us emotionally, it is always going to be very frustrating and deeply depressing, will always be hard to come out of such a harrowing situation, because it's our own folks who have bitten us.

....

Article title "**Consequence of Prejudice**" describes: "Like the wide variety of prejudices that exist in societies around the world, the consequences of the prejudices and the behaviour influenced by them are similarly varied. Prejudice affects the everyday lives of millions of people across the globe. Prejudice held by individuals unnaturally forces on others who are targets of their prejudice a false social status that strongly influences who they are, what they think, and even the actions they take. Prejudice shapes what the targets of prejudice think about the world and life in general, about the people around them, and how they feel about themselves. Importantly, prejudice greatly influences what people expect from the future and how they feel about their chances for self-improvement, referred to as their life chances. All of these considerations define their very identity as individuals.

People acting out their prejudices causes domestic violence, crime, death, and the loss of billions of dollars in lost productivity, property loss, and expense to society, such as cost of court trials and social services provided to victims including psychological counselling, in dealing with dysfunctional (abnormal behaviour) elements of society. Other prejudicial behaviour, such as male teachers favouring calling on male students in a classroom, may be more subtle (less obvious). But its effect can be just as broad-sweeping as the more violent consequences of prejudice. Opportunities in life are lost and personal relationships damaged when people act upon their prejudice. When not acknowledged and confronted, prejudice negatively impacts the lives not only of the victims, but of those holding the prejudice.

Prejudice can impose very dramatic barriers or invisible barriers on individuals. For example, in the United States, many children are raised with certain beliefs, one being the American Dream. The children are taught if they apply themselves and work hard enough and set their sights on what they want most, they can achieve it by persistence. They are not taught about certain social barriers, such as racial or gender discrimination in hiring or in job promotions, that may present themselves throughout their lives that counter the progress made by solid work habits."......

Consequences of everyday prejudice go beyond simply shaping relationships between people. People are relentlessly assaulted by value judgments based on skin colour, social class, gender, religious affiliation, political views, and so on.

Such constant exposure to ridicule and discrimination leads to a lowered self-esteem. Those subjected to such prejudice become unsure where they belong in society. They develop hatred and anger directed both outwardly at those holding prejudices against them and inwardly for having the supposed traits that attract such prejudices. Such prejudices are destructive of individuals and society. But they extract a hidden cost as well by prohibiting individuals from living up to their true potential.

Economic issues are one of the "hot" buttons when it comes to marital stress. Numerous studies show that hard times can increase the risk of divorce as well as **physical abuse** and child neglect. One interesting study of about 80 couples found men were more hostile towards their wives when they were under economic strain and less likely to be warm and supportive. Not surprisingly, this made women less satisfied with the marriage. In other words, one reason you're feeling so disconnected from your husband could be because he's disconnected from you and isn't treating you with the support and warmth you need to feel loving. Furthermore, stress can decrease sexual desire in both men and women. To reconnect emotionally and sexually, it is important to consciously recognize that both of you have been struggling to cope with the stress of finances. This creates a bond between the two of you and allows you to team up—"us against the world" instead of you against your partner.

Then you can purposely plan activities that are exciting and inexpensive and reminds you of happier, more carefree times. What activities did you enjoy together? For instance, if you both loved biking, then take an afternoon bike ride.

Very small but harmful prejudicial actions can create barriers for entire populations, such as women or minorities, seeking to enjoy the benefits of participating in mainstream society. Often these actions are unintentional, caused by prejudices a person is little aware he has. However, many times they are intentional acts meant to degrade another person considered inferior. It is sometimes difficult to determine if an act is unintended and simply insensitive or meant as intentional hostility. Regardless of intentions, the consequence of action is often the same. Many times the person who is the target of such prejudicial actions is placed in difficult situations. Any protest he or she might make of such prejudicial actions would give the appearance of oversensitivity and possibly incite further reaction from the initiator. For example, a woman may be placed in an awkward situation when she is congratulated for offering a solution to a technical engineering problem as if such an idea would not be normally expected of a woman.

When faced with tough problems, men become non-communicative so they can work out how best to help themselves, while women become communicative so that others can work out how best to help them. Men like to demonstrate their abilities by being allowed to solve problems without interference; women like to demonstrate their feelings by being allowed to relate problems without interference.

When men do communicate, they like to get to the point, and generally only want to listen if they feel the conversation has a point; women enjoy talking for its own sake, and are happy to listen unconditionally.

Most people go through life without ever understanding the key elements that make their relationships succeed or fail. The purpose of writing this Book is to shed some light on this very important subject.

Sure, there are a few lucky souls who naturally succeed at interpersonal relationships. But that tiny group probably doesn't include you or me! If we're going to succeed in this challenging arena, we're going to have to do it the hard way. We're going to have to learn from our mistakes and find out what really works. Then we're going to have to stop doing the things that don't work and start doing more of the things that do.

Here are some interesting excerpts from Article title "**Why Men Can't Say No to Women**" giving perspective of men's subtle sexual desire, what men feels and thinks about women; "You've probably heard it a lot in your life – on the news, in magazines, from your friends and probably from your ex-girlfriends: *Men can't say no to sex*. It's often presented as the excuse for many things, from marital infidelity to assault, but is it really true?

Are men just animals, powerless against any remotely attractive woman who comes across our path? Why do we sometimes act that way?

The secret behind why men can't say no to women is simply that we can, but there's too much pressure (both internal and social) not to.

Social Expectations & Sexual Needs

Always being in the mood for sexual conquests is part of the social performance of masculinity, which means it's how everyone thinks men are supposed to be, so that's how most men act.

If you don't want to have sex with a woman, there's an ingrained fear it will reflect on your masculinity, your heterosexuality, or your ability to perform.

If you think that being ready at all times is part of what makes you a man, it can be hard to say no. How does this apply to the dating world?

Well, if you're saying yes all the time (to women/sex), it makes it a lot harder to find out what you really want.

Here's an interesting tidbit on this topic from **PsychologyToday.com**;

"After months of reading and compiling results, the answer was clear. There is a substantial difference, and men have a much stronger sex drive than women. To be sure, there are some women who have frequent, intense desires for sex, and there are some men who don't, but on average the men want it more.

Every marker we could think of pointed to the same conclusion. Men think about sex more often than women do. Men have more sexual fantasies, and these encompass more different acts and more different partners."

But Not Every Woman!

Another problem with men's ability to say no is the fact that nobody likes the feeling of having to reject someone. No matter how high your sex drive may be, you're not going to spark with every woman you meet, and sometimes that has nothing to do with how attractive she is.

If you try to force yourself to feel the desire to sleep with a woman when you don't really have it, you're causing a rift between your mind and your body.

You're wasting time trying to assert your masculinity when you could be meeting someone you do feel genuinely attracted to and could be interested in for more than just sex.

So if you're out with a woman and you're just not feeling it, it's okay to say so. Be kind about it, but be firm enough to ensure you're not sending mixed messages."......

Article title **"Men are From Mars, Women are from Venus"** writes: "Men love to have their abilities recognised and appreciated, and hate to have them scorned or ignored; women love to have their feelings recognised and appreciated, and hate to have them scorned or ignored. Men don't rate feelings highly as in their view they can result in hotly impassioned, wildly unstable behaviour; women don't rate abilities highly as in their view they can result in coldly dispassionate, aggressively competitive behaviour.

Men like to work on their own, and exercise their abilities by solving problems quickly and singlehandedly; women like to co-operate, and exercise their feelings through interactive communication with one another. Men value solutions, and view unsolicited assistance as undermining their effort to solve problems alone; women value assistance, and view unsolicited solutions as undermining their effort to proceed interactively. Men desire that their solutions will be appreciated; women desire that their assistance will be appreciated.

When faced with tough problems, men become non-communicative so they can work out how best to help themselves, while women become communicative so that others can work out how best to help them. Men like to demonstrate their abilities by being allowed to solve problems without interference; women like to demonstrate their feelings by being allowed to relate problems without interference.

When men do communicate, they like to get to the point, and generally only want to listen if they feel the conversation has a point; women enjoy talking for its own sake, and are happy to listen unconditionally.

How to Motivate the Opposite Sex;

A man's instinct is to look after himself, even if it means sacrificing others; a woman's instinct is to look after others, even if it means sacrificing herself. In a relationship, a man has to learn how to care for his partner rather than sacrificing her needs in favour of his own, and a woman has to learn how to be cared for by her partner rather than sacrificing her own needs in favour of his, so that the needs of both are met. If they do this successfully, both win, unlike their instinctive behaviours where one person gains from another's loss. This has to be worked at, because if either partner feels their efforts towards the relationship are not being successful in pleasing their partner, they may feel hurt and decide to revert to their instinctive behaviour. Unfortunately this then causes the other partner to do the same, and the relationship unravels inexorably.

In a relationship, a man needs to feel that his attentions are needed, and a woman needs to feel that her needs are attended. To achieve this, a man has to express his desire to fulfil her needs and her worthiness to receive his care, and a woman has to express her desire for his care and his worthiness to fulfil her needs. Both must remember to appreciate, accept, and forgive the other, and avoid blaming them when they fail."………

There is no doubt that the effects of the use of rape as a weapon of war are effects far-reaching regardless of time, place or culture. Short and long-term support and treatment for victims is substantially lacking, which will only serve to exacerbate the use of rape as weapon of war. Thus an end to the perception that rape is a common and unavoidable tactic of war must occur, making it unequivocally unacceptable. In order to do this there are three main areas of focus which must be in place:

1) One the issue of gender inequality and bias must be removed in all countries, when such programs are in place at peace time it will significantly reduce the stigma and use of rape and gender-based violence in times of conflict.
2) Two, there must be a unified international response to ban the use of rape as a weapon of war once and for all, and thus strategies of prevention and awareness must be put into place, including in internally displaced persons and refugee camps and in times of post conflict.
3) Three, impunity must come to an end, or victims will continue to remain silent and not seek medical, psychological and legal attention if they feel there is no retribution or care for which they are safe to receive.

Something that the compulsive sex offender must know:

1. Sex, as great as it is, can never be a substitute for feelings of value and self-worth. Your sexual identity is critical but you are not your vagina or penis.
2. Relationships exist for mutual sharing not for bullying, coercing or dominating the will of another.
3. It is important to respect your partner's sexual choices and preferences.
4. Catering to your partner's sexual needs, as well as having your own needs met, is critical to a balanced relationship.
5. A difference in sex drive is not an excuse for infidelity; relationships must be built on compromise and trust from both individuals.
6. Your partner is not responsible for "giving you an orgasm". Your sexual climax is primarily dependent upon your own thinking and feelings about sex, as well as on the understanding of how your body responds.
7. Withholding displays of love and affection in an attempt to punish your partner is insensitive and immature.
8. Withholding sex or using it as a reward or promise for "good behaviour" demeans the significance of the act to you and your spouse.
9. Expecting 'sex-on-demand' at all costs and fuming or pouting if is not had, is childish behaviour which is completely unattractive and is likely to negatively impact your marriage.
10. An addictive/compulsive dependence on sex, may signal a need for counselling or therapy.

11. Kindness and thoughtfulness, as genuine displays of affection, can be the most powerful precursors to a sexually satisfying relationship.

Chapter 3

Now the sexual terrorist doesn't actually hold a weapon to your head to have sex; at least not a physical one. Through the use of "emotional weapons" like overt demands, manipulations, angry complaints, put downs, threats, and the withdrawal of attention/affection; sexual terrorists attempt to control the sexual relationship so as to ensure that their every sexual demand is met. In an extreme scenario, violence could also be used. The sexual terrorist is more obsessed with his/her own needs than with a relationship which focusses on meeting the needs of their partner. Now before you accuse me of being a backward thinker, I have no problem with sexual assertiveness or with the celebration of individual sexuality. I am not suggesting that it is not important to desire sexual pleasure and fulfilment but if sex is all that defines a relationship what will happen if or when that desire starts to wane? Moreover, if sex is going to be all about one individual's needs at the expense of another's happiness, why don't people just masturbate and call it a day?

Sexuality in our postmodern age has most decidedly taken on an assertive have-my-needs-met-at-all-costs bent which screams at us from the covers of most magazines. While in some respects this may be great and should guard against things like sexual abuse in relationships, as with any new movement, too far-east, is usually west. Yes, I am most definitely all for personal empowerment and the like but as a counsellor and observer of human behaviour, I am seeing a quality which for the purposes of our discussion I will name "sexual terrorism."

Without having to fully dissect the topic of masturbation, some of us know intuitively that as instructive as some may tout masturbation to be, it could never be enough. The experience of sexual release does not take care of the problem of relational loneliness and the desire for meaningful human connection. So why don't the sexual terrorists among us get this? To be fair, some of us may just have been born with a selfish streak, which turns up, guns blazing, in our intimate relationships. Others may have had failed sexual encounters in the past which sort of "spoiled" them and made them intent never to be left wanting again. Others, through poor modelling, may just believe that being sexually assertive means catering to "Numero uno". Some with deeper emotional issues may even use sex as a form of escapism, resulting in obsessive/compulsive/addictive sexual behaviour. This can take its toll on the other partner who may lack sleep or adequate rest, as a result of these seemingly unquenchable demands.

It is believed according to some scientific research studies that we modern Humans appeared on this planet Earth some 200 Thousand years ago. What makes humans different from animals? No creature is able to create and express humour, not only does humour requires creativity, humour also requires to detach oneself from one's surroundings to see odd, surreal or ironic, humans have ability to observe, describe and appreciate all kinds of beautiful things what nature has created.

We humans make moral judgement and moral choices, our thoughts in this way lifts our thinking to different level and enhances our power of imagination that helps us become creative and to think positively about our desires, human-beings however negotiate conflict through socially created values and codes of conduct.

All emotions are held in our body and have been experienced since we were conceived. They are made up of all our own experiences as well as those of all our ancestors and passed down via the memory of each generation.

As we go through life, we generally only allow ourselves to feel the 'positive' emotions and those which our parents and society approve of. The painful, ugly ones we have learnt to deny....and even some of the happy, spontaneous ones, because we are told they are 'silly and childlike' and they leave us out of control. All emotions are magnetic. Whether we deny them or not. They attract experiences to us to express themselves and to show themselves. Emotions want to be part of our lives all the time.

We hear that thoughts create our reality, which is partly true, but what we don't hear is that thoughts are a secondary representation of our emotions. It is the emotions that drive it all. This is why so many positive thinking practices don't work.

ALL our emotions are projected upon the world and others. We literally SEE the world as we FEEL it inside. We do this without realizing. It is automatic. And emotions attract and create events and circumstances to provide similar emotions to those we are holding inside, whether they are denied or not. This is guaranteed and the function of this law is to show us our TRUE emotions in the deepest part of ourselves, both the suppressed and the allowed ones. It is the most beautiful gift we have been given: the law of attraction.

Is life difficult? Yes indeed, this is a greatest truth, but there are people in this world who enjoy hardship, there are people who are not at all scared of difficulty and are confidently ready to meet and accept any and every challenge, then, there are also people who are extremely scared of difficulty and unable to cope with pressure situations, call them cowards if you like, but people who are scared of difficulty such people mostly prefer to stay in comfort zone and to ensure their safety they do not hesitate but are always ready to make ridiculous compromises to keep trouble away from them.

It's normal to feel apprehensive when you try doing something new and different or when you have to face new challenges. Stepping out of the comfort zones and making yourself uncomfortable taking few odd risk can potentially give big rewards. To achieve greater success in life a person needs to initially go through a difficult phase as it is in time of adversity people get great ideas and power to execute those great ideas, which ultimately gives major peace and self-satisfaction when that person gains incredibly higher success in life. So, this is what life is all about, we never know what the end consequences will be of what we intend doing today, it's just that we need to take decisions and make choices of doing things we want to do.

In life, worldwide most people overwhelmingly concentrates mainly on improving their vocabulary and perfecting communication skills, nothing wrong with it, yes, it is always good to have good communication skills and be a good orator, so, what's missing? Well, even more important is, which apparently, sadly, not many people around the world focuses on or bother about, which is developing good **Listening Skills**. Yes, the crux of most problems in the world for the mankind is because most people have rather poor and appalling Listening skills, bad listening characteristic and mannerism of humans can cause and is causing unprecedented and devastating long lasting pain in most us life. Bad listening skills confounds peculiar types of problems and differences of opinion among individuals, leads to arguments and relationships break-ups. The crux of **Domestic Violence** is because people are less attentive among themselves and do not adhere to and listen to each other well.

Have a assertive and positive approach, differences and contentious issues needs to be sorted out amicably through dialogue and cordial discussions, one very important lesson to learn in life is, never to **Argue**, arguments normally have devastating consequences, arguments destroys image and gives bad reputation, arguments strains relationships or even causes breakup of relationships, be it in personal life, professional or business life, always avoid arguments.

There are many things that happen to us in our life that we react to. It could be something as simple as a fall or as complex and heartbreaking as losing someone we love. When painful circumstances cut into our lives, we remember that pain and do whatever it takes to keep it from happening again.

To protect ourselves from future harm, we may avoid things, places, and circumstances. In the face of the unknown and uncertain, we might be over-protective, cautious, and fearful. Our decisions, goals, and plans center around what we worry might happen. We even try to control all the minute details of our lives in the hopes that we can keep ourselves and the ones we love safe.

Many of us also develop life habits and patterns out of the reactions to the circumstances in our lives. These patterns can take many forms and wear many different hats. From the things we choose to eat or not eat, to the places we live or don't live; from the relationships we keep or don't keep, to the way we spend or don't spend our money; from the way we keep our homes to the way we raise our children; from the way we express ourselves to the way we use our time, all of these things can develop as reactions to the circumstances of our lives.

Why? What drives us to spend (money) too much even when we seem to make all the right moves? The answers seem to lie in psychological impulses and blind spots that are tough for people to recognize, let alone overcome, in their day-to-day lives.

People's mental wiring, for instance, is great at forecasting future income but terrible at imagining future expenses, leading us to set unrealistic budgets. How we think about our emotional resources also matters: If people imagine willpower as something that's limited, they feel the need to reward themselves with things like impulse purchases when they accomplish a goal. And sometimes people unconsciously place such a high value on seeming financially responsible that they end up making choices that cost more money—like making big purchases on credit instead of tapping savings.

One plank of a successful financial plan is an estimate of future income and expenses. The general goal, of course, is to spend no more than you bring in. But too often, the mind gets in the way.

The problem: For reasons researchers are still trying to understand, people are terrible at estimating outflows. **According to a 2008 study in the journal Organizational Behaviour and Human Decision Processes,** humans use overly simplistic reasoning patterns that focus too much on inflows to estimate everything from how much water might be in a tub to the volume of greenhouse gases in the atmosphere. When planning future finances, researchers have found, people think about income (inflows) but don't really focus on rising expenses (outflows) so they end up thinking they can afford things they can't. "This is how people end up buying a house or a car that they ultimately can't afford,"

Power of thoughts is the most powerful tool we humans have, it all depends, how we use it, some do not use it at all, some use it for all the wrong reasons and others who use it for more productive and meaningful reasons and purposes they are the ones who brings positive development in world and helps in development of humans.

Have your own perspective and challenge your perspective, which will help you take appropriate decisions.

Be Positive, think, talk and behave Positively, your Positive body language and talks will help people around you feel more confident in you and they'll trust you, Positive thinking and thoughts will render positive energy to you, Positive thinking of yours will result in Positive outcomes.

Negative thinking and thoughts will make you pessimist, talking, thinking and behaving negatively will make people around you nervous and sceptical, Negative thoughts and thinking will give sleepless nights that will also negatively impact your health, a person whose thoughts and beliefs are negative it as well results in negative outcomes.

What people need to have the most? It is to have a quality "**Analytical Skills,**" to solve complex and uncomplicated problems.

Smart person learns from his/her own mistakes, smarter/smartest person learns from others mistakes.